"As ambassadors from heaven, we must speak the language of our Kingdom. Tongues is our native language. We emphasize perfect prayers with perfect faith, our heavenly language, to navigate these end times. Robert Henderson's book will give you the jump start you need!"

Sid Roth, host, *It's Supernatural!*

"Robert Henderson offers a sound biblical perspective and fresh insight on the call for Christians today to practice the gift of tongues. Get ready to go deeper into the things of God and experience the life-transforming power of the Holy Spirit!"

Dr. Ché Ahn, founder and president, Harvest International Ministry; founding and senior pastor, Harvest Rock Church, Pasadena, CA; international chancellor, Wagner University; founder, Ché Ahn Ministries

# THE GIFT OF TONGUES

# THE
# GIFT

## OF

*Tongues*

WHAT IT IS, WHAT IT ISN'T
AND WHY YOU NEED IT

# ROBERT
# HENDERSON

### Chosen

*a division of Baker Publishing Group*
Minneapolis, Minnesota

© 2021 by Robert Henderson

Published by Chosen Books
11400 Hampshire Avenue South
Bloomington, Minnesota 55438
www.chosenbooks.com

Chosen Books is a division of
Baker Publishing Group, Grand Rapids, Michigan

Printed in the United States of America

Library of Congress Cataloging-in-Publication Data
Names: Henderson, Robert, author.
Title: The gift of tongues : what it is, what it isn't and why you need it / Robert Henderson.
Description: Minneapolis, Minnesota : Chosen, a division of Baker Publishing Group, [2021]
Identifiers: LCCN 2020053988 | ISBN 9780800799687 (trade paperback) | ISBN 9780800762315 (casebound)| ISBN 9781493431298 (ebook)
Subjects: LCSH: Glossolalia.
Classification: LCC BT122.5 .H46 2021 | DDC 234/.132—dc23
LC record available at https://lccn.loc.gov/2020053988

Cover design by Rob Williams, InsideOut Creative Arts, Inc.

21  22  23  24  25  26  27      7  6  5  4  3  2  1

If not for Pastor James Walker and his influence in my life, this book would never have materialized. His selfless pursuit of the Lord and the ministry of the Holy Spirit opened the door for me to experience the power of the Holy Spirit and the gift of tongues. Though he came from a traditional religious position, he laid that aside, with all its advantages, to embrace what he understood to be the life of the Spirit and the gifts He endows. For this, I am eternally grateful.

# CONTENTS

9

# FOREWORD

Robert Henderson has blessed the Body of Christ with a truth that needs to be emphasized in this day and hour. You will find here a thorough biblical presentation of God's purpose for giving the saints the gift of the Holy Spirit, which includes the "other tongues" of our spirit language. Most Full Gospel ministers rarely teach their members about this gift of the Holy Spirit.

Both Robert and I, however, fully recognize the vital importance of this gift. In 2008, God revealed that the third and final church reformation had been decreed. I wrote a book concerning this third reformation and all that it will fulfill of God's end-time purposes in and through His Church. God then spoke to me about writing a book that would enlighten and enable Christ's Church to do that, and the result was *70 Reasons for Speaking in Tongues*, because it gives 70 beneficial reasons for using this particular gift of the Holy Spirit.

God the Father's greatest gift for the world was His only begotten Son, who came to purchase His Church with His own blood. Jesus' greatest gift to His Church was the Holy Spirit.

The Holy Spirit's greatest gift to individual saints is the ability to pray in a spirit language.

During the Pentecostal movement, many books were written on the baptism of the Holy Spirit with the evidence of speaking in tongues. After the charismatic renewal, hardly any books were written on speaking in tongues. We thank you, Robert, for obeying the Holy Spirit's motivation in you to write this book on tongues. We pray that it will go to many in the Body of Christ so that they will be enlightened and motivated to help bring about the great awakening and end-time harvest. Every Christian needs to read and practice these great truths about the value, importance and benefits of using the Holy Spirit's gift of tongues.

> Bishop Bill Hamon, bishop, Christian International Apostolic-Global Network; author, *70 Reasons for Speaking in Tongues*, *God's Weapons of War* and *Your Highest Calling*

# *One*

# WHY THE DEBATE?

It does not take an in-depth search of the Bible to discover the gift of tongues and see it in operation. Numerous Scriptures back this gift up and affirm it, and together we will look at many of them. Yet even Bible-believing people debate about whether or not this gift is for today. As a result of all the debating and questioning, many believers consider the gift of tongues obsolete and archaic. They feel that theologically, emotionally and intellectually, there is no need for this gift in today's world or Church.

I would assert, however, that nothing could be further from the truth. Both in my experience and from a strongly theological viewpoint, I would assert that operating in the gift of tongues holds great advantage for us, and that it is even necessary to living a full life of satisfaction and effectiveness. This is what I will endeavor to illustrate as we progress through the information I will present here regarding this gift.

First of all, what are *tongues*? This gift of tongues is the supernatural ability to speak a language you have never learned, using this language for spiritual and heavenly reasons. Chronologically, the first place we see tongues mentioned in Scripture is Mark 16:17: "And these signs will follow those who believe: In My name they will cast out demons; they will speak with new tongues." We are told here that new tongues are one of the signs that will follow a believer. Believers who have been born again are supposed to be able to manifest and demonstrate the supernatural power of God. This is quite evidently an uncommon experience for many of us today. So often, we seem powerless and without any real authority. Yet we are told that these signs should follow us.

The Greek word for *sign* in this verse is *semeion*, and it means "an indication."[1] The root word it comes from is *sema*, which means "a mark." When we connect these two parts of the definition, it could be said that a *sign* is a mark we carry that indicates we are a believer. We will look into this Scripture from the gospel of Mark in greater depth in a moment, but suffice it to say here that we are supposed to be marked with the supernatural of God. *Tongues* are one of these *markings* or *indications* that we are believers and belong to Him.

As believers, we are supposed to be characterized by the supernatural. Isaiah 8:18 tells us that as God's children, we were made to function in and live from the supernatural power of God: "Here am I and the children whom the LORD has given me! We are for signs and wonders in Israel from the Lord of hosts, who dwells in Mount Zion." The writer of Hebrews in the New Testament would later pick this verse up and record it in Hebrews 2:11–13, making the case from this Scripture that the same DNA and nature that was in Jesus is now in us as those joined to Him:

1. Note that the definitions I provide of Greek and Hebrew words throughout are all taken from *Strong's Concordance*, Orion Systems Version 3.0.3 (2010–2017), https://itunes.apple.com/dm/app/strongs-concordance/id405005619?mt=8.

For both He who sanctifies and those who are being sanctified
are all of one, for which reason He is not ashamed to call them
brethren, saying:
"I will declare Your name to My brethren;
In the midst of the assembly I will sing praise to You."
And again:
"I will put My trust in Him."
And again:
"Here am I and the children whom God has given Me."

When we are told that the One who sanctifies (Jesus) and the
ones who are being sanctified (us as believers) "are all of one,"
it means that we are all the sons and daughters of God. In
other words, the same nature that is in Jesus is now in us. As a
result of our new birth and salvation experience, we now carry
the nature of God Himself. Notice that in Isaiah 8:18, as His
children we are "for signs and wonders." Signs and wonders
are part of our portion as the ones who now carry the nature
and likeness of God. We are here to demonstrate the Kingdom
of God in the earth as believers marked with the supernatural
of God.

## Manifesting the Kingdom

Mark 16:17, the Scripture we looked at that speaks of these
signs following believers, reveals another interesting factor. The
word *follow* is the Greek word *parakoloutheo*, which means
"to follow near." The supernatural realm of God is supposed
to be very close to those of us who are believers. We are not
only supposed to speak of the Lord and His Kingdom; we are
also supposed to manifest it.

This is what the apostle Paul said in 1 Corinthians 4:20: "For
the kingdom of God is not in word but in power." If all we have

is a gospel of *word*, or of reasoning and no demonstration, we are falling far short of God's original intent for us as believers. We are to manifest signs of the supernatural. It is these signs that will convince the world of the reality of who Jesus is.

Signs are to follow very near to us. We must position our faith and believe God for the supernatural in which the Bible says we are to operate. We cannot let a powerless Christianity fashion us. Paul warned us of this in 2 Timothy 3:5, saying some people would live their life "having a form of godliness but denying its power." Then he told us, "And from such people turn away!" Paul calls Christianity without power merely a form of godliness, and he makes the extremely strong statement that we should get away from those who claim to be Jesus' people but have no evident power in their life.

*We are to manifest signs of the supernatural. It is these signs that will convince the world of the reality of who Jesus is.*

Wow, if we were to take this word at face value, there would be a mass exodus from much of Christianity today. I am not advocating this. I understand that there are other ideas we need to consider. This does tell us how desperate we should be, however, for a Gospel of power and not just word. We are to go after this realm of signs and wonders following us. They are not a luxury; they are an absolute necessity for us as believers. We must not settle. We must set our hearts in agreement with God's Word, until our experience as believers lines up with the Word. This is our portion as the children of God.

One of these signs following us as believers is the gift of tongues. I would be so bold as to say that the gift of tongues is absolutely essential to walking in and demonstrating this supernatural power I have been speaking about. We will see this more as we progress. The word *tongues* in the Greek is the word *glossa*. By definition, it means "a language, especially one naturally unacquired." In other words, we did not acquire this language through natural means. The ability to speak and function in the gift of tongues came from a supernatural encounter. Out of this supernatural encounter, the power and ability to speak and pray in tongues became present in us.

## My Experience with Tongues

I first experienced this gift myself many years ago. Through a series of events, my family came into what has since been referred to as the "charismatic renewal." This was a time from the 1960s well into the 1980s when people were encountering the Person of the Holy Spirit in new and powerful ways. The strict religious structures of many denominations were being challenged by the impact of the Holy Spirit and His gifts on people. One of these gifts was the gift of tongues.

Our family ended up leaving the denominational church we had been part of for decades, if not centuries. As a result of my father's hunger for the supernatural, we found ourselves in one of these new charismatic churches. Its pastor had been removed from the traditional church he had led, all because of his encounter with the Holy Spirit on a new and powerful level. My dad and several other members of my family began to experience the Holy Spirit on these new levels as well, and began to speak in tongues.

As a twelve-year-old boy, I would watch this in hunger myself, even longing to have the same encounter. I remember one time when I was left in the back seat of the car while my mom went in the house. I decided I would try to speak in tongues, as I had heard others do. I could not do it. I was unable to make the sounds that would have been associated with a tongue or prayer language. I vividly remember this. It affirmed to me that I did not have the gift of tongues and that speaking in tongues was not just something I could do from a desire or natural ability.

I don't really remember how much time passed after that incident, but later on I was in a service where people who wanted the gift of tongues were being prayed for. Because of my previous attempt in the car, I was aware that I could not pray in tongues from my own ability, so I went forward for prayer. As others prayed for me, I began to speak. To my amazement, a supernatural language I had never learned began to flow out of my mouth. It actually caught me by surprise because of my failure to speak in such an unknown language when I had tried it on my own.

From that time until now, the result has been that I have a gift of tongues I operate in, and I speak in tongues regularly. It has been and continues to be a strong and powerful influence in my life. For forty-plus years, I have been learning about the power of this gift. I would say irrevocably that this gift of tongues has been as big a blessing in my life as anything else I have ever encountered. It is a true gifting from the gracious hand of God into the lives of those who hunger and thirst for Him.

## Tongues of Men and Angels

When we talk of tongues, we should know that they can be languages of earth or of heaven. The apostle Paul alluded to this in 1 Corinthians 13:1 when he said, "Though I speak with the tongues of men and of angels, but have not love, I have become sounding brass or a clanging cymbal." Even though his emphasis is on operating in love, Paul also gives us some insight into tongues. He shares that tongues for the believer can be from languages known in the earth among men, or from languages unknown that are angelic and heavenly in nature.

This is why we must be careful in judging too harshly what our gift of tongues or someone else's gift sounds like. We might hear someone speak in tongues and think it sounds like nothing from this earth. That could be exactly right, because it could be a tongue of angels. Clearly, from what Paul declared, not only are there earthly languages we might speak supernaturally even though we don't know them; there are also angelic languages we might be speaking.

Acts 2:4 chronicles the initial infilling with the Holy Spirit of 120 believers, which resulted in the gift of tongues: "And they were all filled with the Holy Spirit and began to speak with other tongues, as the Spirit gave them utterance." The result was that other people who were listening, who spoke various languages in the natural, all heard these believers speaking of the glory of God. Verses 6–8 show that as these believers spoke in tongues, they were actually speaking the different languages of their listeners, which they had no way of knowing:

> And when this sound occurred, the multitude came together, and were confused, because everyone heard them speak in his own language. Then they were all amazed and marveled, saying to one another, "Look, are not all these who speak Galileans? And how is it that we hear, each in our own language in which we were born?"

People from many other countries and regions heard these Galilean believers speaking in a wide variety of "home dialects." This is because the supernatural gift of tongues that the believers had received in the Upper Room on the Day of Pentecost came forth in earthly languages. These 120 believers, now filled with the Holy Spirit, were speaking tongues in the languages of men, which enabled their hearers afterward to understand them.

Several years ago, when I was pastoring in a small town in Texas, I brought in a guest speaker who was Haitian. In Haiti, French is a common language because of the French heritage and influence there. Our guest speaker had stayed on after his time of ministry, and he came to our morning prayer time the next day. As we were praying, I would speak in the gift of tongues and intermingle it with my native language of English, which is a common practice for me. When we were through with the hour-long prayer time, this Haitian man approached me and asked if I knew French. I assured him that I did not. He then began to tell me that every time I would speak in tongues and finish a time of praying, I would say the words *je t'aime*, which in French means "I love you."

I was astounded at this. I realized that I had been saying "I love You" to the Lord in a language I did not know. Not only was it a language I did not know; it was also one of the languages considered the most romantic in the earth. I was telling the Lord through tongues "I love You" from the deepest parts of my heart.

Many people who experience the gift of tongues recount that it is as if their natural language is insufficient to express the deepest cry of their heart to the Lord. Through the gift of tongues, they are able to release from their spirit that which is longing for the Lord Himself. The Holy Spirit uses this gift of tongues to help us release the cry of our heart, filled with His passion, to God.

As we have seen, there can be times when such tongues are not of this earth; they are of the heavenly dimension. I believe one of the reasons God allows this is so heaven can come to earth. When we speak a language of heaven, the atmosphere of heaven can begin to permeate the atmosphere of earth.

One of the greatest mandates Jesus left us was to pray heaven into earth. Matthew 6:9–10 tells us to pray until heaven's atmosphere begins to dominate the realms of earth: "In this manner, therefore, pray: Our Father in heaven, hallowed be Your name. Your kingdom come. Your will be done on earth as it is in heaven." When we are empowered to pray in an angelic tongue, if it in fact brings the atmosphere of heaven into earth, this mandate is accomplished. A tongue that we share with the angels allows the atmosphere they create to become the atmosphere we encounter. What an awesome thing! This can be just one of the reasons we might be empowered to speak with the tongues of angels, as well as the tongues of men.

*The Holy Spirit uses this gift of tongues to help us release the cry of our heart, filled with His passion, to God.*

## No Need for Tongues?

With all of this said, then why the debate over whether or not tongues are relevant and even theologically applicable for today? Throughout my history of walking with the Lord and functioning in ministry, I have encountered at least three ideas that allow resistance to tongues and their operation. The first idea is that we no longer have the need for tongues today. The second idea is that this gift is actually the work of the devil. The third is that tongues are illogical and unintelligible. Let's look at each of these objections to tongues in more detail.

First, why would some modern-day believers maintain that we no longer need the gift of tongues today? These people say that in the beginning of the Church, tongues were necessary to spread the Gospel. As we saw in Acts 2, the disciples were able to speak in the language of other cultures. But now, those who oppose this gift insist that such an ability is no longer necessary since we have the Bible available in almost all languages. We also have the ability to translate from language to language in both speech and the written word. The miracle of tongues such as operated on the Day of Pentecost is therefore now unnecessary, say those who hold to this idea.

I believe people who say this are missing the point. The miracle occurred on that day not just so a group of people could hear the Gospel in their own languages. In fact, the Bible doesn't even say they were hearing the Gospel. Acts 2:11 clarifies that they were hearing the disciples speak about the works of God: "We hear them speaking in our own tongues the wonderful works of God." To me, this means that it was not so much a Gospel message the listeners were hearing, as it was praise, honor and glory being given to God for His favor and grace. In the Greek, the word translated "wonderful works" here is *megaleios*. It means "magnificent, conspicuous favor." In other words, the disciples were praising God for His glorious grace.

Ephesians 1:6 reflects this cry of adoration and glory, "to the praise of the glory of His grace, by which He made us accepted in the Beloved." This could have been what the believers who were speaking in languages they did not know were saying. They were resounding the glory and majesty of the conspicuous grace and favor that had come on their lives through the power of the Holy Spirit. Even though their minds did not know what they were saying, their spirits were rejoicing in the adulation of God and His kindness. Through the gift of tongues, they then were erupting forth with praise to the One who had endowed them with such wonders.

My question to those who say we no longer need this gift of tongues is, Why wouldn't we need it? Who would deny the power of something so glorious touching our lives? That there would be such a praise lifted to God that people all around would stand in wonder! People who would deny us such an experience tell us that we no longer need tongues because that which is perfect has come. First Corinthians 13:10–11 does speak of something perfect coming that will do away with something partial:

> But when that which is perfect has come, then that which is in part will be done away.
>
> When I was a child, I spoke as a child, I understood as a child, I thought as a child; but when I became a man, I put away childish things.

Those who resist the validity of tongues for today say that what is perfect has come, and that this is a reference to the canon of Scripture, or the Bible. Their argument is that because we now have the inerrant Scriptures, we no longer have the need for tongues or even the other gifts.

This argument has many holes. Even though I believe that the Bible is indeed the inerrant Word of God, I do not believe this Scripture is speaking of that idea. Neither do I understand that since we are now mature and need to put away childish things, this would include tongues and other expressions of gifting. Yet some believers would contend that since we have now matured as the Church throughout the millennia, we have no need for these gifts.

Nothing could be further from the truth. I would say that we have as much—or more—need of the Holy Spirit's gifts today as on the Day of Pentecost. We need like never before the power, authority, anointing and gifts of God to empower us in

*I would say that we have as much—or more—need of the Holy Spirit's gifts today as on the Day of Pentecost.*

the culture we are contending for. In fact, when Paul penned these words about the perfect coming, he was not talking of the Bible being that which was perfect. He was, in fact, speaking of a perfect love that would come. Let's look at this entire Scripture in context. When perfect love, which is Jesus Himself, comes, then there will be no more need for that which is partial:

> Love never fails. But whether there are prophecies, they will fail; whether there are tongues, they will cease; whether there is knowledge, it will vanish away. For we know in part and we prophesy in part. But when that which is perfect has come, then that which is in part will be done away.
>
> When I was a child, I spoke as a child, I understood as a child, I thought as a child; but when I became a man, I put away childish things. For now we see in a mirror, dimly, but then face to face. Now I know in part, but then I shall know just as I also am known.
>
> And now abide faith, hope, love, these three; but the greatest of these is love.
>
> 1 Corinthians 13:8–13

When we stand face-to-face with Jesus in perfect love, only then will tongues cease and there will be no more need for the gifts. Until that time, we desperately need the empowerment that comes with tongues and other expressions of the Holy Spirit. Only when the perfect love of God has fully come will we no longer need tongues. We are not there yet. We will not be there until the Second Coming of the Lord. Then, all that He has graciously deposited in us as His people will be invalidated.

That which is in part will no longer be needed, because His fullness will have come! So biblically and theologically speaking, tongues *have not* passed away. We have not yet left the dispensation of time when they are still needful, because that time will only end when Jesus returns.

## A Devilish Language?

A second objection leveled against the gift of tongues is that it is of the devil. I have actually heard this idea more than once through the years. It seems that when people cannot explain something logically, then it must be of Satan. Jesus warned us about attributing the works of God to the devil. He actually classified it as the unpardonable sin.

Matthew 12:24 shows the religious leaders of Jesus' day claiming that His ministry of casting out devils was through the power of the devil. When the Pharisees heard about a deliverance He had done, their response was, "This fellow does not cast out demons except by Beelzebub, the ruler of the demons." When Jesus heard this, He began a discourse explaining why it could not be true. He showed that what He did was through the power of the Holy Spirit, and He addressed how you cannot remove a strong man from his house unless a stronger man comes upon him. Basically, Jesus was declaring that through the power of the Holy Spirit, He was stronger than any demonic force. Then He made this powerful and serious statement:

> Therefore I say to you, every sin and blasphemy will be forgiven men, but the blasphemy against the Spirit will not be forgiven men. Anyone who speaks a word against the Son of Man, it will be forgiven him; but whoever speaks against the

Holy Spirit, it will not be forgiven him, either in this age or in the age to come.

Matthew 12:31–32

Jesus was saying that when you attribute the works of the Holy Spirit to Satan, you are getting dangerously close to blasphemy against the Holy Spirit, for which there is no forgiveness. I do believe that when men with sincere hearts make judgments in ignorance, that is one thing. I understand that God is merciful and kind. If, however, people whose motives are not pure seek to hold on to their place and resist God's work through such statements, that is another thing, and I believe it can be treacherous ground.

We must be very careful in this area. We should be slow to judge something as being of Satan before we know for sure, especially when it is purported to be of God and the power of the Holy Spirit. As I said, I have heard people claim that tongues are of Satan. Some of these people were simply ignorant. With other people, however, I could sense a demonic agenda that was driving them not to enter into the operation of this gift themselves, as well as driving them to seek to keep others from entering into the deeper things of God.

Jesus accused the religious leaders of His day of just that, speaking out strongly to them: "Woe to you lawyers! For you have taken away the key of knowledge. You did not enter in yourselves, and those who were entering in you hindered" (Luke 11:52). *Woe* was an exclamation of grief. In other words, there was no hope for these people. We must be very careful about how we approach supernatural demonstrations. We should move with caution in evaluating them until we know for sure about them. This includes tongues and making any declaration that they are from the devil.

26

## Unintelligible Gibberish?

The third objection or point of debate against the gift of tongues is that it is not logical or intellectual. Some people who have heard others speak in tongues call it unintelligible gibberish. This gift somehow or other offends their minds and/or intelligence. This is not a valid argument, either. As we have seen, sometimes tongues are from the earth's known languages, but other times tongues can be angelic in nature. If we are judging and criticizing tongues because we don't like the way they sound, we might be speaking evil of an angel's language. Just because something does not seem to impress us on earth does not mean it isn't valid and good.

The other thing to remember is that God takes what seems foolish to confound the wise. First Corinthians 1:27–29 tells us that God loves to take what mankind does not esteem and use it to work His purposes:

> But God has chosen the foolish things of the world to put to shame the wise, and God has chosen the weak things of the world to put to shame the things which are mighty; and the base things of the world and the things which are despised God has chosen, and the things which are not, to bring to nothing the things that are, that no flesh should glory in His presence.

Sometimes God allows tongues to sound foolish, yet they are filled with great power in their operation. Just because this gift does not make sense to our natural man does not mean it isn't of God. One of the main reasons the Lord does this kind of thing is so that He gets the glory for all things. No flesh can take credit. It is to His praise when what humankind seems to despise, He uses in powerful ways.

So it can be with tongues. So much power is locked up within this gift. We will discover this reservoir as we move forward, and we will know God's closeness as we learn to function in the gift of tongues!

*Two*

# THE PERSON OF
# THE HOLY SPIRIT

It is impossible to understand the gift of tongues and its power without understanding the Holy Spirit and His operation. It is clear in Scripture that the ability to speak in a language we have not learned naturally is the result of the Holy Spirit filling our life. Several places in Scripture unveil this truth. It is the Holy Spirit who empowers this occurrence. Acts 2:1–4 shows without question that it is the Spirit who comes upon and operates within a person to bring about this phenomenon:

> When the Day of Pentecost had fully come, they were all with one accord in one place. And suddenly there came a sound from heaven, as of a rushing mighty wind, and it filled the whole house where they were sitting. Then there appeared to them divided tongues, as of fire, and one sat upon each of them. And they were all filled with the Holy Spirit and began to speak with other tongues, as the Spirit gave them utterance.

Being filled with the Holy Spirit is what precipitated the power to speak in other tongues. This means we should understand who this Spirit is. (We will talk more about that in a moment.)

Another place that we see this kind of occurrence is in Acts 10:44–46. As Peter is preaching and states his testimony before Cornelius and his household, without warning the Holy Spirit comes upon all those who are there. It is as if the Holy Spirit interrupts Peter's well-designed speech with His demonstration and presence:

> While Peter was still speaking these words, the Holy Spirit fell upon all those who heard the word. And those of the circumcision who believed were astonished, as many as came with Peter, because the gift of the Holy Spirit had been poured out on the Gentiles also. For they heard them speak with tongues and magnify God.

Up until this time, the power and Person of the Holy Spirit had only been seen coming upon the Jews. Peter and the other Jewish people with him are amazed that God is pouring out His Spirit on the non-Jewish, Gentile people. Notice that Peter and the rest knew this was the Holy Spirit because they heard the new believers speak with tongues and magnify God. Tongues were the manifestation of the Holy Spirit's presence and power in this situation.

Acts 19:6 is one other place where we see the Holy Spirit's presence being made known because of tongues in operation. The apostle Paul is ministering to the people in Ephesus, and he administers the Holy Spirit to them through the laying on of hands: "And when Paul had laid hands on them, the Holy Spirit came upon them, and they spoke with tongues and prophesied." Again, please notice that when the Holy Spirit shows up, these believers begin to speak in tongues. On this occasion, however, they also prophesy, which is another manifestation of the Holy Spirit and His presence. *Prophesying* is not only a *foretelling*; it is also a *forthtelling* of something through people, from God. In other words, the Holy Spirit empowers us to speak in an encouraging way whatever God might presently be saying.

In 1 Corinthians 14:3, Paul helps us understand one of the most prevalent dimensions of prophecy: "But he who prophesies speaks edification and exhortation and comfort to men." *Edification*, *exhortation* and *comfort* are all words that have to do with encouragement and affirmation. These things are one of the main purposes of prophecy. When the believers at Ephesus spoke in tongues and prophesied, they were speaking from the Holy Spirit in an unknown language, and also speaking in their native tongue. The unknown language was referred to as *tongues*, while what they spoke in the known language of their culture was called *prophecy*, which came forth through the act of them *prophesying*.

## The Holy Spirit Is God

We can see clearly that the ability to speak in an unknown language called *tongues*, and even to prophesy, comes from the empowerment of the Holy Spirit. So who is the Holy Spirit? If we are to come into cooperation with Him, we should know and understand some things about Him. Paul actually said in 1 Corinthians 12:1–2 that he did not want us to be *ignorant* concerning the Holy Spirit and His operation: "Now concerning spiritual gifts, brethren, I do not want you to be ignorant: You know that you were Gentiles, carried away to these dumb idols, however you were led." The word *gifts* is not actually in the original text, which means Paul was saying that he did not want us to be ignorant of the spiritual dimension, or the movement and operation of the Holy Spirit.

Paul then points out that in their former life, these believers served *dumb* idols. This word in the Greek is *aphonos*, meaning to be "voiceless." Paul was pointing out that they had served idols and gods that were incapable of speaking. Now, however, we serve a *speaking God with a voice*. The gifts or manifestation of the Holy Spirit involves the Lord *speaking* to us and through us. This includes tongues. If we are to see a true and powerful revelation of the Holy Spirit in us and through us, we must not be ignorant of these things. Having an idea of who He is and how He operates is essential and is of great benefit.

> The gifts or manifestation of the Holy Spirit involves the Lord speaking to us and through us. This includes tongues.

Understanding different aspects of the Holy Spirit can help us greatly. The first thing we should know is that the Holy Spirit is *God*. This might sound like an obvious and even unnecessary thing to state, yet many people do not have an appreciation for the Holy Spirit as God. He quite often is therefore not honored, esteemed or worshiped the way He should be. The result can be that He is not free to move among us, and even worse, that He is quenched, grieved and even blasphemed (three sins against the Holy Spirit that we will discuss further shortly). The Holy Spirit is the Third Person of the Trinity. He is an equal of the Father and Son. He is the One who is in the earth today, *applying* all that Jesus died for us to have. Without Him, there would be no application of all Jesus did for us on the cross.

Many Scriptures show that the Holy Spirit is completely God. One, however, stands out to me above the rest. When

Peter confronts Ananias and Sapphira in Acts 5:3–4, he clearly shows this important aspect of the Holy Spirit:

> But Peter said, "Ananias, why has Satan filled your heart to lie to the Holy Spirit and keep back part of the price of the land for yourself? While it remained, was it not your own? And after it was sold, was it not in your own control? Why have you conceived this thing in your heart? You have not lied to men but to God."

Peter at first accuses Ananias of lying to the *Holy Spirit*. Then, however, he says Ananias lied to *God*. This is because the Holy Spirit is God. Some would believe that the Holy Spirit is inferior to God, or maybe that He is a "junior God." However, *He is God*. This is important, because otherwise we treat Him with less honor and worship than we should. When we realize that the Holy Spirit is God, we will begin to respect, honor and worship Him with the weightiness He is due. This allows an even greater manifestation of who He is to work among us. As someone once said, "When we treat God as God, He acts like God among us."

On one occasion a few years back, I was in a high-profile service where the power of the Holy Spirit touched me in a tremendous way. Many from the church I led were among the thousands who witnessed this. As we were boarding the bus to go home, some people began to comment about it in an innocent, yet very vocal way, joking about what they had seen. An associate at the host ministry had accompanied me to the bus, and he overheard what they were saying. When he heard their laughter, he quickly and firmly chastised these people for it, telling them, "You must never dishonor the power and movement of the Holy Spirit among you, or treat it lightly."

I was quite honestly astounded. I had not been offended at all by the people responding the way they did to what they had seen. I knew these people loved me and were in their own way acknowledging what had happened. Yet this man who had upbraided them was correct. In the midst of the people simply commenting and joking, there was a subtle lack of respect for the Holy Spirit and His power among us. After all, if Jesus Himself had appeared and touched me instead of the Holy Spirit, would we have acted the same way? I doubt it.

## Guarding against Overfamiliarity

Since the Holy Spirit is unseen, sometimes we don't carry the honor and worship that we should toward Him. We also don't appreciate His activities toward us. Because He is so good and brings God's love and care to us, we frequently can become very familiar with His operation. This is a deadly act and a subtle motivation we must guard against. Our overfamiliarity with the Holy Spirit can allow us to respond to Him in a less honoring way than we would other manifestations of the Lord and His presence. When this happens, our lack of honor and worship toward the Holy Spirit *will* cause a diminishing of His activities among us. But the more we honor and worship Him, the more He will move among us and reveal the Lord's glory.

We must fight against this sense of overfamiliarity with the Holy Spirit. Overfamiliarity is what created a spirit of unbelief that would not allow Jesus to do miracles in Nazareth. Mark 6:3–6 unveils the story of Jesus coming to this city where He had grown up, only to find that an overfamiliarity with who He and His family were had created unbelief in the people. This caused a lack of honor for Him that would not allow Him to manifest His power among them. The people of Nazareth were asking each other, "Is this not the carpenter, the Son of Mary, and brother of James, Joses, Judas, and Simon? And are not His sisters here with us?" (verse 3), and they were even "offended at Him." Look at Jesus' response to their questioning (verses 4–6):

> But Jesus said to them, "A prophet is not without honor except in his own country, among his own relatives, and in his own house." Now He could do no mighty work there, except that He laid His hands on a few sick people and healed them. And He marveled because of their unbelief. Then He went about the villages in a circuit, teaching.

In Nazareth, the people's unbelief had its roots in overfamiliarity. This kind of familiarity is in a sense a curse that restricts God from manifesting among us. It is a curse in that it cuts us off from that which the Lord desires us to have. It takes faith to embrace the Lord and His movement in our midst. If there is no faith, it places a very strong limitation on the Lord. We are actually told that *limiting* God is a grievous thing. Psalm 78:40–41 shows that when the people of God placed limits on Him as Lord, it provoked and grieved Him: "How often they provoked Him in the wilderness, and grieved Him in the desert! Yes, again and again they tempted God, and limited the Holy One of Israel."

Limiting the Lord and what He desires to do is a serious thing. We do this through our unbelief, which is what happened in Nazareth. Jesus could do nothing there but heal a few sick people. This same Jesus, empowered by the Holy Spirit, had done and was doing signs and wonders of tremendous proportions in other places. Yet in Nazareth, as a result of the people's unbelief He could do none of those. Wow! The lack of power was not because the Lord did not want to move. The lack of power was because of the people's unbelief, born out of overfamiliarity with Jesus and His natural family. This familiarity had the result in them of *not* esteeming Jesus as God.

The same is true with the Holy Spirit. If we become so over-familiar with Him and His presence that we cease to acknowledge Him as God, we risk shutting down what He can do among us, even though He desperately desires to move. Galatians 4:13–16 gives us insight into this:

> You know that because of physical infirmity I preached the gospel to you at the first. And my trial which was in my flesh you did not despise or reject, but you received me as an angel of God, even as Christ Jesus. What then was the blessing you enjoyed? For I bear you witness that, if possible, you would have plucked out your own eyes and given them to me. Have I therefore become your enemy because I tell you the truth?

Paul reminds the Galatian church of the way they had esteemed him in the beginning of his ministry among them. Now, however, that esteem, respect and honor has been replaced with familiarity. He reminds them that at first, they treated him the way one would treat an angel. Then Paul actually says no, really they treated him with the same honor they would have given Jesus Himself. Notice that he connects the blessing this church enjoyed to the *way* they received him. This is a powerful idea— a concept we must get. We can only receive from that which we honor.

Notice also that honor is joined to giving. The people's honor of Paul made them give in a sacrificial way. Paul declared that they would even have given their eyes to him. This is either a metaphor for extreme, extravagant giving, or Paul had bad eyesight and was referring to their heart for him in the midst of his disease and infirmity. Either way, the honor they had for Paul made them want to help him and give in an extra-special way. Paul wonders why this honor has now been replaced with the idea that perhaps he is their enemy, and why they no longer value him the way they had before. An overfamiliarity had crept in that was polluting the way they accepted Paul—and therefore what they could receive from him.

We see in the next verse what at least part of the culprit was that had allowed this to happen: "They zealously court you, but for no good; yes, they want to exclude you, that you may be zealous for them" (Galatians 4:17). There are other people seeking to influence the Galatian believers and win their hearts away from Paul. These people desire to break the honor and esteem the Galatian church has for Paul, lessening Paul's effect and replacing his influence with theirs. Notice that by means of their *courting* the believers, these others seek to *exclude* or *isolate* the Galatians.

Of course, when I hear the word *court*, I immediately think of the dating ritual that usually occurs before two people decide to marry. The purpose when you court as a couple is to get to know each other and discern if the two of you are right for each other. This courting time can allow two people to fall in love. During the courting period, people make great efforts to impress their chosen one and convince that person how great married life will be. Many times, however, getting a true sense of what married life will be like is impossible during this time. This is because bad things are hidden and excluded from sight. A temper, sullenness, control issues, irresponsibility, laziness and other negative things about one person or the other are unseen because these traits are kept behind the scenes. Often, the whole purpose of the courting period becomes hiding the negative and highlighting the positive. This usually makes for some difficulties that a couple will face once married.

Paul is actually warning the Galatians that the people who are courting them will come to "no good." As the Galatians come under their control and domination, these people will isolate them and cause them to be excluded. Paul is speaking specifically of those "courters" who were wanting to live under the Law of Moses while still believing in Jesus, and who were wanting others to do the same. Paul warns the Galatians not to leave grace to go back under the law. Yet because of this influence on them, an overfamiliarity had developed toward Paul. He was losing his influence with the Galatians as a result of the ones whom they were allowing to court and affect them.

This same spirit of overfamiliarity that was in Nazareth, creating unbelief in Jesus, was also at work in Galatia against Paul and his ministry. The truth is that overfamiliarity is a human reality. When we are around people regularly, we become familiar with them. This is often why a pastor may become less effective than he or she desires. It is not because the pastor is not anointed. It is because the people have become overfamiliar with the pastor and have stopped honoring him or her in their hearts. Then some traveling guest comes along who brings a word or ministry that seems to supersede that of the pastor. Everyone is astounded by this new face and voice. It is not because this new person is more anointed. It is simply because the people are showing the new person an honor that allows them to receive on a different level. They are not overfamiliar with this person; therefore, they are able to draw from him or her on a higher level.

This same problem can happen in a marriage where the two partners begin to take each other for granted through overfamiliarity. They become so accustomed to each other that they stop honoring one another. This can be a prelude to trouble in a home. Where there is no active honor and value of the other person, problems will arise. We must guard against the spirit of overfamiliarity in this and in our other relationships.

## Three Sins against the Holy Spirit

I have discussed all of this to say that this is what happens when we do not see the Holy Spirit *as God*. When we do not value, treat and worship Him as such, we greatly diminish His ability to affect us and transform us through His power. The thing that can preserve us from this trap is the *fear of the Lord*. Remember that since the Holy Spirit is God, He is to be reverenced, valued, esteemed and feared as God.

> *Remember that since the Holy Spirit is God, He is to be reverenced, valued, esteemed and feared as God.*

We are told in Acts 9:31 that the early Church walked in the fear of the Lord and the comfort of the Holy Spirit: "Then the churches throughout all Judea, Galilee, and Samaria had peace and were edified. And walking in the fear of the Lord and in the comfort of the Holy Spirit, they were multiplied." Notice that the *fear of the Lord* preceded the *comfort of the Holy Spirit*. In other words, these early believers had a right respect for the Holy Spirit as Lord, and therefore the comfort and closeness of who the Lord is was among them.

The word *comfort* in the Greek is *paraklesis*. It means "to console" and "to call near." As we walk with a healthy perspective of who God is, we experience a closeness of His presence with us through the Holy Spirit. If we do not value the Holy Spirit as God, however, we will be guilty of three sins the New Testament speaks of against the Holy Spirit. These sins are the result of not seeing the Holy Spirit *as God*, and they involve *grieving* Him, *quenching* Him or *blaspheming* against Him. Let's examine each of these briefly.

The first sin against the Holy Spirit is *grieving* Him, which Ephesians 4:30 tells us not to do: "And do not grieve the Holy

Spirit of God, by whom you were sealed for the day of redemption." The word *grieve* here is the Greek word *lupeo*. It means "to distress or make sad." If you were to look at the context of this verse, you would find that it talks about being careful with our words, avoiding stealing and engaging in other activities that result from living a holy, clean life. When we as believers don't live a life of holiness, we grieve the Holy Spirit of promise. This results in what we might call conviction. When we do something wrong, the Holy Spirit's grief over it will be made manifest to us. We will lack the peace and well-being that normally accompanies those who are walking in agreement with the Spirit. This sense of conviction comes because we are grieving the Holy Spirit through our attitudes, actions and thoughts.

If we will pay attention to this conviction, the Holy Spirit will keep us out of those things that make Him sad and distressed. This will allow us to perfect holiness in the fear of the Lord, as 2 Corinthians 7:1 declares: "Therefore, having these promises, beloved, let us cleanse ourselves from all filthiness of the flesh and spirit, perfecting holiness in the fear of God." As we walk daily with the Lord and His Holy Spirit, He will perfect us in holiness. Through the empowerment of the Spirit, we will be delivered from the filthiness of flesh and spirit as we seek not to grieve Him through our conduct.

The second sin against the Holy Spirit is *quenching* Him, which 1 Thessalonians 5:19 tells us not to do, admonishing us to keep the flame of the Holy Spirit alive and ignited: "Do not quench the Spirit." The word *quench* in the Greek is *sbennumi*, meaning "to extinguish and go out." This is the idea of putting a fire out. The Holy Spirit is a fire. He creates passion and power in us. John the Baptist declared that Jesus would baptize us with the Holy Spirit and fire. "I indeed baptize you with

40

water," John said, "but One mightier than I is coming, whose sandal strap I am not worthy to loose. He will baptize you with the Holy Spirit and fire" (Luke 3:16). The Greek word for *fire* here means "lightning." John the Baptist was promising that when Jesus sent the Holy Spirit into our lives, the firepower of lightning would ignite us. When we are told not to quench the Spirit, we are being admonished not to put that fire out, which is meant to burn hot and flaming.

This fire burning speaks to us of the gifts and manifestations of the Holy Spirit in operation. When we grieve the Holy Spirit, we are offending His holy character. When we quench Him, we are shutting down His desire to manifest Himself in power and glory through His gifts and endowments. To avoid quenching the Spirit, we must allow ourselves to be vessels He can flow through. We cannot shut down His desire to reveal the Lord because we are afraid, intimidated or even uncertain. Our moving in faith and being willing to take risks is essential to avoid quenching the Holy Spirit and His movement in us and through us. This is true of moving in the manifestations of the gifts found in 1 Corinthians 12.

The third sin against the Holy Spirit is *blaspheming* against Him. All the sins against the Holy Spirit are serious, but this one is the most serious. Matthew 12:24–32 gives us clear insight into what this sin involves:

> Now when the Pharisees heard it they said, "This fellow does not cast out demons except by Beelzebub, the ruler of the demons."
>
> But Jesus knew their thoughts, and said to them: "Every kingdom divided against itself is brought to desolation, and every city or house divided against itself will not stand. If Satan casts out Satan, he is divided against himself. How then will his kingdom stand? And if I cast out demons by Beelzebub, by whom do your sons cast them out? Therefore they shall be your

41

judges. But if I cast out demons by the Spirit of God, surely the kingdom of God has come upon you. Or how can one enter a strong man's house and plunder his goods, unless he first binds the strong man? And then he will plunder his house. He who is not with Me is against Me, and he who does not gather with Me scatters abroad.

"Therefore I say to you, every sin and blasphemy will be forgiven men, but the blasphemy against the Spirit will not be forgiven men. Anyone who speaks a word against the Son of Man, it will be forgiven him; but whoever speaks against the Holy Spirit, it will not be forgiven him, either in this age or in the age to come."

As I mentioned earlier, the religious leaders of Jesus' day attributed what He was doing to the powers of the devil. In addressing this, Jesus was declaring that when we attribute the power of the Holy Spirit to the workings of Satan, we can be getting very close to blasphemy against the Holy Spirit! This sin, we are told, will not be forgiven in this life or in the one to come. This is because God arises to defend the Holy Spirit, who will not defend Himself. The Holy Spirit's job is to reveal the Father and the Son. He does not talk of Himself, according to John 16:13–14:

> However, when He, the Spirit of truth, has come, He will guide you into all truth; for He will not speak on His own authority, but whatever He hears He will speak; and He will tell you things to come. He will glorify Me, for He will take of what is Mine and declare it to you.

As a result of the Holy Spirit not defending Himself, God the Father and God the Son arise in great defense of Him. This is why the punishment for speaking against the Holy Spirit and His activities is so great. It therefore behooves us to be very careful about what we judge as not being of God. The Lord has always confounded people when it comes to who He is and how He moves. Even Jesus' coming did not happen the way the Jews had envisioned that their Messiah would come. The result was that they rejected Him even though numerous prophecies had pointed to His coming in such a way.

The bottom line, however, is that these Jewish leaders actually accused Jesus of doing miracles through the power of Satan and his forces. This was blasphemy against the Holy Spirit, according to Jesus. This sin will not be forgiven in this life or in the one to come. This is why we must be so careful as we evaluate phenomena that we encounter. Just because something does not line up with our presupposed religious ideas does not mean it isn't of God.

Sometimes God comes in ways that offend our minds, so that He might get to our hearts. Even the gift of tongues can fall into this category. My entire Christian life, I have heard the argument that the gift of tongues and its "gibberish," as some would call it, have no value. Yet if this gift is really from God, we must be very careful. It is one thing to say it isn't real. It is quite another to claim it is from the devil. When we make that claim, we could be getting very close to the blasphemous sin we are discussing. Just because something makes no logical sense to us, that does not mean it isn't God. His ways are not our ways, as Isaiah 55:8–9 declares:

> "For My thoughts are not your thoughts, nor are your ways My ways," says the LORD. "For as the heavens are higher than the earth, so are My ways higher than your ways, and My thoughts than your thoughts."

The way we think, evaluate and judge here in the earth may not be the way God does so from heaven. We must walk gently and softly before the Lord, making room for the possibility that there may be things we don't know. We need a child's heart that is easily convinced of God's ways. Look what Jesus said in Matthew 11:25–26:

> I thank You, Father, Lord of heaven and earth, that You have hidden these things from the wise and prudent and have revealed them to babes. Even so, Father, for so it seemed good in Your sight.

According to Jesus, God actually hides things from those who are wise and prudent in their own eyes. The religious and those who think they have everything figured out miss out on the wonders of the Lord. Yet the Lord loves to reveal these things to the babes, or to those who see themselves as dependent on His goodness. These are the hungry ones who have yet to develop a critical, cynical view that would cause them to dismiss what their minds cannot compute. These are the babes, and God loves to reveal His secrets to them. If we will have this kind of babe's heart, we will never be guilty of blaspheming the Holy Spirit. This perspective will keep us free from judging something our minds have difficulty computing and placing it in a category that we would consider as not being of God.

## Walking in Communion with God

Another Scripture that shows the equality of the Holy Spirit as God is 2 Corinthians 13:14, which speaks of God, Jesus and the Holy Spirit, and also of the influences that flow from each One: "The grace of the Lord Jesus Christ, and the love of God, and the communion of the Holy Spirit be with you all. Amen." Grace flows out of who Jesus is. Love flows from the heart of God as the Father. Notice, however, that there is a *communion* with God that the Holy Spirit provides.

The Holy Spirit desires to bring us into intimacy with God. Remember that He will not talk of Himself. He will take what belongs to the Father and to Jesus and show it to us. This means that through the communion and closeness of the Holy Spirit's presence, the secrets of God are revealed to us. First Corinthians 2:9–10 shows us that the Holy Spirit makes known to us unimaginable things:

> But as it is written:
>   "Eye has not seen, nor ear heard,
>   Nor have entered into the heart of man
>   The things which God has prepared for those who love Him."
> But God has revealed them to us through His Spirit. For the Spirit searches all things, yes, the deep things of God.

The Holy Spirit takes the deep things of God, the hidden things of God, and unveils them to us. This happens as we walk in communion with Him. The word *communion* in the Greek is *koinonia*. It means "a partnership, fellowship, a distribution." So when we walk in communion with the Holy Spirit, we are partnering with Him. There are things we can do together with Him that we cannot do by ourselves.

We definitely need the Holy Spirit, but He also needs us. I remember a time when the Lord moved and people were healed in a meeting I was leading. After the meeting, I said to the Lord, *Thank You so much for what You did.*

Immediately, I heard the Lord say back to me, *Thank You for walking with Me in such a way that allowed Me to do it.*

> *The Holy Spirit takes the deep things of God, the hidden things of God, and unveils them to us. This happens as we walk in communion with Him.*

Wow, I had never had that thought before! The power of the Holy Spirit is able to work because we are walking in a communion with Him that creates a partnership. The result can be the Lord manifesting Himself.

Here is a final Scripture for us to look at that shows how the Holy Spirit is God, just as the Father and Son are:

> Now the Lord is the Spirit; and where the Spirit of the Lord is, there is liberty. But we all, with unveiled face, beholding as in a mirror the glory of the Lord, are being transformed into the same image from glory to glory, just as by the Spirit of the Lord.
>
> 2 Corinthians 3:17–18

This Scripture clearly says "the Lord is the Spirit," which is equating the Holy Spirit to being God. When we encounter the power and presence of the Lord through the Holy Spirit, we are encountering God. We must treat the Holy Spirit as the Lord who He is. As we do that, we can be transformed into His very image. The Holy Spirit takes the realms of who God is and shows them to us. The result is that we become like Him more and more. The very power and presence of the Lord, administered by the Holy Spirit, touches us and changes us from glory unto glory. As we with *unveiled face* behold Him—meaning that we are hiding nothing—we are changed.

The Holy Spirit fashions, molds, heals and empowers us to be more like Jesus. Believe it or not, much of this process is released and accommodated as we learn to pray in the gift of tongues. This gift unlocks the supernatural life of the Spirit to move in us and through us, as we will learn even more about in the chapters yet to come.

*Three*

# THE BAPTISM OF
# THE HOLY SPIRIT

As you will see, we cannot talk about the power of the gift of tongues without talking about *the baptism of the Holy Spirit*. This is actually a New Testament idea and term. John the Baptist first mentioned it in describing what Jesus would do when He came. John was baptizing people in water, but he declared that Jesus, as Messiah and Savior, would baptize them in the Holy Spirit. Look again at what John said in Luke 3:16:

> John answered, saying to all, "I indeed baptize you with water; but One mightier than I is coming, whose sandal strap I am not worthy to loose. He will baptize you with the Holy Spirit and fire."

It was one thing to put someone under water naturally, in a symbolic way. It was something else for the Holy Spirit to come upon a person. The first could be considered a natural and religious activity. The second, however, is of supernatural effect. John the Baptist was emphasizing that Jesus' ministry would be done through the power of the Holy Spirit. Just as John had baptized people in water, Jesus would baptize people in the Holy Spirit.

The word *baptize* in this passage is the Greek word *baptizo*. It means "to immerse, submerge, to be fully wet." John was letting it be known that even as he placed people completely under the water in his ritual of baptism, Jesus would completely submerge us in the power, authority and Person of the Spirit of God. Jesus actually referred to this as "the Promise of My Father" (Luke 24:49). After His resurrection, He appeared to the disciples and opened their understanding, letting them know what He had accomplished through His death, burial and resurrection. He also let them know that the baptism of the Holy Spirit, called the promise of the Father, was going to empower them:

> Then He said to them, "Thus it is written, and thus it was necessary for the Christ to suffer and to rise from the dead the third day, and that repentance and remission of sins should be preached in His name to all nations, beginning at Jerusalem. And you are witnesses of these things. Behold, I send the Promise of My Father upon you; but tarry in the city of Jerusalem until you are endued with power from on high."
>
> Luke 24:46–49

Because of what happened on the Day of Pentecost, we know that the promise of the Father was a reference to the baptism of the Holy Spirit. As I talked about in chapter 2, we see in Acts 2:1–4 what happened as the Holy Spirit entered the Upper Room where the disciples were gathered. The promise of the Father, otherwise referred to by John the Baptist as the baptism of the Holy Spirit, overwhelmed them, and they began to speak in other tongues, as the Holy Spirit granted them utterance.

Why is this awesome experience referred to as the promise of the Father? There are several reasons, but allow me to mention an important one. Throughout the Old Testament, God had promised there would be people empowered and anointed by the Holy Spirit. During Old Testament times, only a handful of prophets, perhaps as well as a few priests and kings, had experienced the closeness of God's presence and Spirit. The Lord had promised, however, to pour out His Spirit on all flesh. Joel 2:28–29 is one of the most prominent places where He made this promise:

> And it shall come to pass afterward that I will pour out My Spirit on all flesh; your sons and your daughters shall prophesy, your old men shall dream dreams, your young men shall see visions. And also on My menservants and on My maidservants I will pour out My Spirit in those days.

In this Old Testament passage, the Lord is promising a wholesale release of the Spirit of God upon human culture. This did happen in the New Testament, which is why Peter pointed out this Scripture from Joel when the Holy Spirit fell in the Upper Room in Jerusalem (see Acts 2:16–21). He used this passage from the Old Testament to pinpoint and explain what was happening in the moment. The Father's promise from the Old Testament had arrived. God had poured out His Spirit upon *all flesh*, and not just a handful. The anointing and power of the Holy Spirit was now accessible to all.

## The Person and Presence

From that day until now, this is still true. The Holy Spirit, though always active in the earth, is now here in a new way. He is here to empower those who belong to God, with His *Person* and *presence* coming upon those who desire Him and are hungry for Him. The presence of the Holy Spirit is the assurance and sign that we belong to the Lord. Galatians 3:14 seeks to explain that whoever is in faith and believes in Jesus is included in the *seed of Abraham*, "that the blessing of Abraham might come upon the Gentiles in Christ Jesus, that we might receive the promise of the Spirit through faith."

Although we may not be Jews naturally, we are esteemed as being in covenant with the Lord. We are grafted into the vine and are now included as being from the lineage of Abraham. As a result of this, the power of the Holy Spirit belongs to us. Grafted into Abraham's lineage, we are able to receive the power of the Holy Spirit through faith. We become part of Abraham's seed and are confirmed in this through the Holy Spirit. Wow! The power and Person of the Spirit is available to us because we believe in Jesus as the Messiah and Savior of the world.

We also see that this anointing and power of the Holy Spirit is for us because He belongs to God's covenant people. In Exodus 30:25, we see God's directive to make an *anointing oil*. This oil is symbolic of the Person of the Holy Spirit and His effects on our life: "And you shall make from these a holy anointing oil, an ointment compounded according to the art of the perfumer. It shall be a holy anointing oil." Exodus 30:33 then tells us that this anointing oil was not to be placed on an outsider or someone who was outside the covenant of God: "Whoever compounds any like it, or whoever puts any of it on an outsider, shall be cut off from his people." This declaration lets us know that only those who are in covenant with the Lord will receive the anointing and power of the Holy Spirit. This anointing is not to be placed on an outsider.

This is what the New Testament also tells us. The Person of the Holy Spirit is the assurance and guarantee that we belong to the Lord. As 2 Corinthians 1:21–22 declares, we have been given the guarantee of the Holy Spirit: "Now He who establishes us with you in Christ and has anointed us is God, who also has sealed us and given us the Spirit in our hearts as a guarantee." We should pay attention to two significant words in this passage, which says the Holy Spirit is a *seal* and also a *guarantee*. The word *seal* is the Greek word *sphragizo*, meaning "to stamp for security or preservation." When the Holy Spirit as the promise of the Father comes into our hearts, He is here to keep us and preserve us for the eternal Kingdom of our Lord. God has commissioned His Spirit to watch over us as those who now belong to Him. The Holy Spirit is to see to it that nothing is lost and that all are delivered to the Father in the end. He is able to keep what has been given to Him to care for and watch over until that Day.

The other word to note here is *guarantee*. It is the Greek word *aarhabon*, meaning "a pledge" or "a part of the purchase-money or property given in advance as security for the rest." The Holy Spirit is given to us as a sign that we have been purchased by the Lord. This would be equivalent in our culture to someone buying a home and putting down earnest money. The earnest money given prior to the full purchase of the home assures the one selling it that the ones buying it are sincere. The buyers' willingness to make an investment of money declares their sincerity and earnestness.

This is what we experience when we receive the Person of the Holy Spirit, which is God giving us the down payment of our full salvation. The Holy Spirit's closeness, presence and empowerment in our lives assure us that God will complete the transaction. There will be a day when we enter the fullness of our salvation. We can be confident of this because of the down payment the Father has made into our lives. If the Holy Spirit is but the down payment of our full inheritance in God, then what kind of glory must await us? We can be absolutely certain that what God has promised, He will fulfill. We can know this because of the Person and power of the Holy Spirit, whom the Father has placed in our lives.

> *If the Holy Spirit is but the down payment of our full inheritance in God, then what kind of glory must await us?*

## Not Just *with* Us, but *in* Us

Another thing we should be aware of is that the Holy Spirit's power to come into the earth and fill us and baptize us in His presence is a result of the work of Jesus. Clearly, there is a difference between the work of the Spirit in the Old Testament and the work of the Spirit in the New Testament. In the Old Covenant, only *special* people had encounters with the Holy Spirit. As I mentioned earlier, the prophets and some priests and kings were anointed with the Spirit. For instance, David cries out in Psalm 51:11, asking God not to remove the Holy Spirit from him: "Do not cast me away from Your presence, and do not take Your Holy Spirit from me." After David's adulterous, grievous sin with Bathsheba, and then the killing of her husband, Uriah, to cover it up, David is afraid that God will remove the closeness of His presence from him. He does not want to lose the Holy Spirit's presence.

Clearly, there were those in the Old Testament who had encounters with and an awareness of the Spirit. He was *with them*. Jesus, however, tells His disciples in John 14:16–17 that the Holy Spirit will not only be *with* them; He will be *in* them:

> And I will pray the Father, and He will give you another Helper, that He may abide with you forever—the Spirit of truth, whom the world cannot receive, because it neither sees Him nor knows Him; but you know Him, for He dwells with you and will be in you.

Jesus promises to petition the Father on the disciples' behalf, so that in Jesus' absence they will have the Spirit of truth, the Helper who will come and be with them—and not just be *with* them, but *in* them. This is the difference between the Old Testament experience with the Holy Spirit and the New Testament experience. In our time, the Holy Spirit comes to dwell in us, because the blood of Jesus has now made us a suitable dwelling place for Him. This is why the Holy Spirit could only be with people in the Old Covenant. The blood of bulls and goats was unable to cleanse them sufficiently so that the Spirit could indwell them. Only the blood of Jesus has this power to cleanse us and make us a dwelling place for the Holy Spirit.

The principle is that the Holy Spirit can only dwell in what the blood has cleansed. When we are born again and the blood of Jesus is speaking on our behalf, the Holy Spirit then has what He needs to be able to take up residence in us. Hebrews 12:24 says we have come "to Jesus the Mediator of the new covenant, and to the blood of sprinkling that speaks better things than that of Abel." The blood of Jesus, speaking on our behalf, allows God the legal right to forgive our transgressions fully, not just roll them away for a year, which is what the blood of bulls and goats did in the Old Testament. This full redemption in us and for us now gives the Holy Spirit the right to come and dwell in us fully. Because Jesus knew what He was about to accomplish on the cross, He could declare to His disciples that the Spirit of truth, the Helper, would come and live *in* them.

Jesus was explicit about the Holy Spirit's coming to earth. He declared that the Spirit could not come until He Himself went away. In John 16:7, Jesus actually tells His disciples that He has to go so He can send the Holy Spirit back: "Nevertheless I tell you the truth. It is to your advantage that I go away; for if I do not go away, the Helper will not come to you; but if I depart, I will send Him to you."

Jesus instructed the disciples that He must leave the planet physically in order for the Holy Spirit to come. I believe there are at least two reasons for this. The first reason involves what we just talked about—a full atoning work needed to be done so the Holy Spirit would have a suitable resting place. Symbolically and functionally, the Holy Spirit has been looking for a place to reside. Remember in the days of Noah, when the flood was yet on the earth and Noah sent out a dove to see if the waters had dried up? Look at Genesis 8:6–12:

> So it came to pass, at the end of forty days, that Noah opened the window of the ark which he had made. Then he sent out a raven, which kept going to and fro until the waters had dried up from the earth. He also sent out from himself a dove, to see if the waters had receded from the face of the ground. But the dove found no resting place for the sole of her foot, and she returned into the ark to him, for the waters were on the face of the whole earth. So he put out his hand and took her, and drew her into the ark to himself. And he waited yet another seven days, and again he sent the dove out from the ark. Then the dove came to him in the evening, and behold, a freshly plucked olive leaf was in her mouth; and Noah knew that the waters had receded from the earth. So he waited yet another seven days and sent out the dove, which did not return again to him anymore.

Obviously, the dove is a picture of the Holy Spirit. The Holy Spirit came on Jesus in Matthew 3:16 as a dove:

> When He had been baptized, Jesus came up immediately from the water; and behold, the heavens were opened to Him, and He saw the Spirit of God descending like a dove and alighting upon Him.

When Noah sent forth the dove, I believe it was a picture of the Holy Spirit looking for a place to rest His feet. The Holy Spirit has been looking and searching for a place, person and/or people to come and dwell in. He first found it in Jesus at the River Jordan. As those cleansed by Jesus' blood, we have also become a place of His presence, where He can live. If you will be open to Him, the dove of God's presence, the Holy Spirit, is yet looking for those who will open their hearts to Him. Because of what Jesus has done, we can now be the place where He can put His feet down.

The second reason Jesus said He had to go away was because He said He would pray to the Father, and the Father would then release the Holy Spirit into the earth. We saw in John 14:16 that Jesus said He would ask the Father for the Holy Spirit on His disciples' behalf: "And I will pray the Father, and He will give you another Helper, that He may abide with you forever." This is why after Jesus' death, burial and resurrection, He had to ascend back to the Father. His ascension back to the Father was essential to the release of the Holy Spirit being poured out upon the disciples.

To fully understand this, we need to recognize that Jesus' death, burial, resurrection and ascension accomplished certain legal matters in the spirit world. All this work Jesus did revoked any legal right the devil could have claimed to stop the Holy Spirit from empowering us. Hebrews 4:14 tells us that

Jesus passed *through* the heavens on His way to the right hand of God: "Seeing then that we have a great High Priest who has passed through the heavens, Jesus the Son of God, let us hold fast our confession." The combination of Jesus' death, burial and resurrection revoked any claims that Adam's sin had granted the devil. Jesus' ascension through the heavens, or the spiritual realm, removed demonic entities from resisting the outpouring of the Holy Spirit on the Day of Pentecost.

So to be clear, Jesus' work on the cross and in the tomb, and His power over death through His resurrection, *revoked* every legal claim Satan had used for generations to resist the coming of the Holy Spirit to indwell believers. Jesus' ascension through the spirit realm, where these demon entities operated from, *removed* them from their functional place where they could hinder and resist. The result was Jesus' ability to receive from the Father a release whereby the Holy Spirit could be poured out on the disciples on the Day of Pentecost, to live *in* them. The Spirit of God was free to empower people again on the same level that Adam enjoyed in the Garden of Eden, prior to humankind's fall from sin.

Acts 1:9 shows the disciples watching Jesus visibly disappear into the clouds and go up into heaven: "Now when He had spoken these things, while they watched, He was taken up, and a cloud received Him out of their sight." They knew that Jesus had disappeared and was gone. After the Holy Spirit fell in the Upper Room in Jerusalem, Peter makes this astounding statement as he seeks to explain all that has happened:

> This Jesus God has raised up, of which we are all witnesses. Therefore being exalted to the right hand of God, and having received from the Father the promise of the Holy Spirit, He poured out this which you now see and hear.
>
> Acts 2:32–33

Jesus received the Holy Spirit from the Father. According to Peter, Jesus then poured out the Holy Spirit upon those in the Upper Room. The coming of the Holy Spirit was *the sign* that Jesus had reached the Father and that He was God, even as He had said. They knew they had seen Him leave, but had He reached the Father? Was He really Jesus, the Son of God? When the power of the Holy Spirit, with the cloven tongues of fire, sat on the disciples' heads and they became filled with the Spirit and spoke in tongues, it forever established the guarantee of who Jesus was, and therefore who they were in Jesus. The coming of the Holy Spirit brought power and authority as these early believers were filled, baptized and indwelt by the Spirit of the living God.

## *Not* the Same Thing

On the Day of Pentecost, then, the Holy Spirit entered the Upper Room after Jesus received Him from the Father and poured Him out. These disciples were baptized in the Holy Spirit, even as John the Baptist had prophesied. As this filling/baptism took place, they spoke in tongues. We have already seen the way Acts 2:4 clearly connects the baptism of the Holy Spirit with the operation of tongues: "And they were all filled with the Holy Spirit and began to speak with other tongues, as the Spirit gave them utterance." One of the main questions people ask is if this baptism of the Holy Spirit is the same as the salvation experience. I would definitely say it is *not* the same thing. Titus 3:4–5 speaks of the regeneration of the Holy Spirit this way:

> But when the kindness and the love of God our Savior toward man appeared, not by works of righteousness which we have

done, but according to His mercy He saved us, through the washing of regeneration and renewing of the Holy Spirit.

We are saved when the Holy Spirit brings a regeneration and a renewing. The word *regeneration* here in the Greek is *paliggenesia*. It speaks of "a renovation through the idea of repetition." When the Holy Spirit comes into our lives, He begins a renovation project. He is committed to bringing us into the full image of who Jesus is. The word *renew* is the Greek word *anakainosis*. It also carries the idea of a "renovation that brings a freshness." Through the washing of regeneration and the renewing of the Holy Spirit, we are transformed progressively into Christ's image. It would appear in Scripture that this is what we would call a salvation experience, or being born again. The Holy Spirit is present and involved in this, or we would not be brought into this newness and freshness of life.

> I liken salvation to being the place and time where I got Jesus and got the Holy Spirit's power and effect. When I received the Holy Spirit, however, and was baptized in Him, He got me!

The baptism of the Holy Spirit, however, is another work—an even deeper work. I liken salvation to being the place and time where I got Jesus and got the Holy Spirit's power and effect. When I received the Holy Spirit, however, and was baptized in Him, He got me! We can see a demonstration of this difference in Acts 19:1–7, where Paul encounters twelve people who are born again but have not received the Holy Spirit's fullness.

And it happened, while Apollos was at Corinth, that Paul, having passed through the upper regions, came to Ephesus. And finding some disciples he said to them, "Did you receive the Holy Spirit when you believed?"

So they said to him, "We have not so much as heard whether there is a Holy Spirit."

And he said to them, "Into what then were you baptized?"

So they said, "Into John's baptism."

Then Paul said, "John indeed baptized with a baptism of repentance, saying to the people that they should believe on Him who would come after him, that is, on Christ Jesus."

When they heard this, they were baptized in the name of the Lord Jesus. And when Paul had laid hands on them, the Holy Spirit came upon them, and they spoke with tongues and prophesied. Now the men were about twelve in all.

Notice that these men were called *disciples*. In other words, they had already been led to the Lord and were born again. This is what the term *disciples* would imply. Yet when Paul asked them if they had received the Holy Spirit, they said they had never even heard of such a thing. This is where much of the Church is today. They are born again, yet they have no awareness of the Holy Spirit and His empowerment that come through being baptized in the Spirit.

When Paul understood that these disciples were not baptized in the Spirit, he began to dig a little deeper. He discovered that their theology was just a little off, due to some incomplete instruction they had received from Apollos. Apollos was a great teacher and thinker, but he had influenced these men before he himself had been instructed fully. Acts 18:24–26 shows us why these men in Ephesus were somewhat stunted in their understanding:

Now a certain Jew named Apollos, born at Alexandria, an eloquent man and mighty in the Scriptures, came to Ephesus. This man had been instructed in the way of the Lord; and being fervent in spirit, he spoke and taught accurately the things of the Lord, though he knew only the baptism of John. So he began to speak boldly in the synagogue. When Aquila and Priscilla heard him, they took him aside and explained to him the way of God more accurately.

Before Aquila and Priscilla got hold of Apollos and helped him with his theology, he had already been with these twelve men in Ephesus. This is why they were baptized into the baptism of John rather than in the name of the Lord Jesus Christ. Although mighty in scriptural knowledge, Apollos did not know about the baptism of the Holy Spirit. Remember, these twelve told Paul that they had not even known if there was a Holy Spirit. As Paul seeks to lead them into the baptism of the Holy Spirit, he corrects their baptism, but more than anything, he corrects their theology. This is important. A wrong theology can keep us out of what God has for us.

Remember how John had said that he baptized with water, but that Jesus would baptize with the Holy Spirit? John's baptism was a baptism unto repentance. In other words, through the act of baptism people were repenting. This, however, is not what Christian baptism is. Christian baptism is recognizing and identifying with who Jesus is and what He has done for us. Christian baptism is embracing Jesus' work for us, not our work for ourselves! When we are baptized, we declare, "When Jesus died, I died with Him. That means my old nature [or old man, as Paul called it] died with Jesus on the cross." Romans 6:3–11 actually explains what baptism is for the believer:

> Or do you not know that as many of us as were baptized into Christ Jesus were baptized into His death? Therefore we were buried with Him through baptism into death, that just as Christ

was raised from the dead by the glory of the Father, even so we also should walk in newness of life.

For if we have been united together in the likeness of His death, certainly we also shall be in the likeness of His resurrection, knowing this, that our old man was crucified with Him, that the body of sin might be done away with, that we should no longer be slaves of sin. For he who has died has been freed from sin. Now if we died with Christ, we believe that we shall also live with Him, knowing that Christ, having been raised from the dead, dies no more. Death no longer has dominion over Him. For the death that He died, He died to sin once for all; but the life that He lives, He lives to God. Likewise you also, reckon yourselves to be dead indeed to sin, but alive to God in Christ Jesus our Lord.

When we were baptized, we were baptized into *His death*, not ours. When we understand the power of baptism, it sets us free. Through baptism, I died with Christ to my old man—yet I also was raised with Him into His newness of life. This was all done for me. Through baptism, I am identifying with what Christ did for me. After my baptism, I then am able to *reckon* these spiritual realities into place. This is an act of faith that draws from realties in the spirit world. It is what Paul was correcting with the twelve men in Ephesus. As they got their theology right, Paul then prayed for them and they received the baptism of the Holy Spirit. As the Holy Spirit came and dwelt in them, they began to speak in tongues and prophesy. It was not either/or. It was both.

As I covered in chapter 2, *prophesying* can be the life flow of God pouring through us by the power of the Holy Spirit, so that we speak forth, or forthtell, the heart and passion of the Lord. His very love, care, encouragement and inspiration strengthen us and others as prophecy flows through our spirit and out of our mouth. Not only did tongues flow through these freshly filled believers, but this prophetic unction the Holy Spirit created in them flowed as well. When these men began to speak in tongues and prophesy, it was a release of the life-giving Holy Spirit flowing through them as they were baptized in Him.

It seems very clear that wherever people were baptized in the Holy Spirit in Scripture, they spoke in tongues. Some people have wanted to do away with this idea or water it down, yet it is clearly a scriptural idea. Whether it is in Acts 2, Acts 10, Acts 19 or Paul's teaching elsewhere on the gifts of the Spirit, tongues always plays an important and unrelenting part. I personally believe that the gift of tongues is something every believer should receive when he or she is baptized in the Holy Spirit. This is because of how powerful tongues are, and also because every place in Scripture where we see people baptized in the Holy Spirit, the gift of tongues is manifest and present.

## Tongues as a River

Biblically, the gift of tongues can be the initial outflow of the Holy Spirit as He fills and baptizes us. Jesus promised that when the Holy Spirit comes into a person, rivers of living water would flow. John 7:37–39 chronicles Jesus inviting and urging those who are thirsty to come:

> On the last day, that great day of the feast, Jesus stood and cried out, saying, "If anyone thirsts, let him come to Me and drink. He who believes in Me, as the Scripture has said, out of his heart will flow rivers of living water." But this He spoke concerning the Spirit, whom those believing in Him would receive; for the Holy Spirit was not yet given, because Jesus was not yet glorified.

Jesus was actually beckoning those who had been through the religious feast, yet still felt empty and dry. He was crying for these to come. He promised that any who came to Him thirsty would drink of the living water that would be theirs through the Holy Spirit. In fact, this Scripture makes it clear that this is what Jesus is referring to. He is inviting all who are thirsty to come to Him and receive the Holy Spirit. The result would be *rivers* of living water flowing from their innermost being.

Notice that Jesus said *rivers*, plural. The gift of tongues is one of those rivers. There are many rivers the Spirit unlocks. Again, it would appear that the gift of tongues is quite often the first river that begins to flow. As the Holy Spirit comes to glorify Jesus in us and through us, the gift of tongues will begin to operate. From the very depths of our spirit, the life-altering, thirst-quenching and deep reservoir of the Holy Spirit will begin to flow. It will erupt out of our spirit and through our mouth, in the form of tongues.

This encounter and experience is for everyone today. The Holy Spirit has come to glorify Jesus and to unleash within the deepest places of our being the life flow of these rivers.

## Thirsting for God Himself

Should you be *thirsty*, as Jesus said, for this life-changing encounter, allow me to help you. How can someone posture himself or herself to receive this immersion/baptism in the Holy Spirit? The first thing is to develop a thirst for God and who He is. People are thirsty for a lot of things. They want gifts from God, breakthroughs from the Lord, the blessings of God and other things that they might be desperate for. As right as these things might be, it is quite another thing to be thirsty for the Lord *Himself*. When we move from not just wanting what

He can do, to wanting *Him*, this is an amazing transition. He will answer this cry.

Hebrews 11:6 tells us that God rewards those who diligently seek Him: "But without faith it is impossible to please Him, for he who comes to God must believe that He is, and that He is a rewarder of those who diligently seek Him." This verse seems to place the emphasis on seeking *Him*. I am not saying that it is wrong or incorrect to seek what the Lord can do. We obviously can and should do this. But when we move to seeking Him and longing for Him, we have positioned ourselves to receive.

Romans 8:32 tells us that God will give us everything when we receive the Lord Himself: "He who did not spare His own Son, but delivered Him up for us all, how shall He not with Him also freely give us all things?" If we are to freely get all things from the Lord, it is because we first get *Him*. The key is to be thirsty for the right thing, which is the Lord Jesus Himself.

Several years ago, I had a prophet come and minister at the church I had raised up and was leading. The presence of the Lord was very close to us in those days, whenever we would meet. After this prophet had been with us for a few days, he said something that grasped my attention. He said to me, "I go a lot of places where people are hungry for the prophetic. However, in this place people are hungry for God."

His assessment was correct. Somehow or other, we had created a culture among us in which we wanted the Lord Himself. We were thirsty for Him. The result was many healings, miracles and manifestations of the Holy Spirit happening among us. We were not necessarily seeking those things; we were seeking the God of those things. I am not saying that we were a special people. I am saying, however, that the Lord had set upon us a grace that allowed this kind of heart in us. We were thirsty for Him, and He was revealing Himself among us.

## Asking to Receive

Another occurrence that demonstrates this thirst for God Himself happened when I was an associate pastor with a particular ministry. One of my jobs was to lead a midweek small group. This group was held in a couple's home who had come from a denominational church that did not believe in the baptism of the Holy Spirit. They had become thirsty for something more than what they had been experiencing. I knew in particular that the lady desired to be baptized in the Holy Spirit. So one night after the meeting had concluded in their home, I prepared to ask her if she wanted me to pray for her to receive the baptism of the Holy Spirit. Suddenly, I heard the Lord say to me, *She must ask.*

I knew then that I was not to ask her if she wanted this baptism in the Spirit. I needed to let her thirst be so great that she would ask. I simply moved on and did not engage her about it that night. The next week at the end of the meeting, she walked up and asked if I would please pray for her to receive the Holy Spirit and His power. This was what the Lord had told me I must allow to happen. Of course, when she herself asked, I said I would pray. I laid my hands on her head, and we simply asked the Lord to baptize her in His Holy Spirit. Without hesitation and with no encouragement from me, she opened her mouth and began to speak. Out flowed a most beautiful language in tongues. She was filled instantaneously and flowed in her new language of worship and adoration to God.

The thing that made this so special for me was that I had prayed for quite a number of people who had struggled to speak in tongues even when they had asked to be filled. Either through fear or uncertainty or even a lack of faith, they would never quite come into the release of the Holy Spirit in them and through them. I was perhaps expecting the same ordeal in praying with and for this lady. Yet her experience was immediate—soft and gentle, yet very powerful and life changing. The difference was *thirst*. She was thirsty. This is why the Lord had me wait until she asked. She needed to get thirsty enough that it would push her past fear, embarrassment, timidity and any other thing that would hold her back. Her thirst for God overwhelmed all these things and allowed her to receive the baptism of the Holy Spirit, with the immediate outflow of speaking in tongues.

Sometimes we experience a lack of results because we are seeking to give something to people that they are not thirsty for. We must ask the Lord to make us and others thirsty for Him. Jesus said that whoever thirsts, He will fill and satisfy. May the thirst of God come upon us for who He is!

So two vital things about being baptized in the Holy Spirit are that first, we must be *thirsty*, and second, we must *ask*. Just as I waited for this lady until she asked, people must ask from the Lord themselves. The Lord will not push Himself or anything from Him on us. We must ask of Him. James 4:2 tells us that many times, we don't have because we have not asked: "You lust and do not have. You murder and covet and cannot obtain. You fight and war. Yet you do not have because you do not ask." Notice that our lack of asking produces attempts in our own ability to obtain things. When these efforts are unfruitful, deep frustration can set in that causes deep resentment and even bitterness of soul. It seems this is what this particular Scripture is referring to.

*Two vital things about being baptized in the Holy Spirit are that first, we must be thirsty, and second, we must ask.*

Notice that the answer is simply to ask. We are told that we don't have because we don't ask. How often we *forget* simply to ask of the Lord, rather than seeking to produce things ourselves. When it comes to receiving the baptism of the Holy Spirit, we definitely should ask. We have already been told that Jesus would baptize us in the Holy Spirit and with fire (see again Luke 3:16). If this is His express word, then we should take Him at His word and ask Him to do this for us. We can have others pray with us for this, and/or we can simply ask for ourselves.

My father received the Holy Spirit and spoke in tongues this way. He was up by himself early one morning, sitting on the hearth of the fireplace in our living room. He was thirsty for God. We had come from a very dry denominational church. My dad wanted something so much more. We had been introduced to the things of the Spirit and the baptism of the Holy Spirit, but no one in our family had received this from the Lord. In these early morning hours, when my dad was by himself, he simply asked the Lord to baptize him in the Holy Spirit. Immediately, he began to speak in tongues as he was there alone with the Lord. This changed his life and the life of our entire family.

The point is, my father *asked*. There is something very powerful about asking in childlike faith of the Lord. We will not be denied when we take Jesus at His word and believe that He will baptize us with freshness and newness in the Person of the Holy Spirit. As important as thirst is to being filled, asking must be added to that thirst.

## Asking in Faith

Matthew 6:7–8 tells us that God knows cry of our hearts even before we ask: "And when you pray, do not use vain repetitions as the heathen do. For they think that they will be heard for their many words. Therefore do not be like them. For your Father knows the things you have need of before you ask Him."

If the Lord knows what I need or want from Him before I ask, then why do I have to ask? It is a matter of faith. God responds to faith, not to need or even desire. There are many people who need things, or even simply want them. This does not move God's heart. Faith in Him and in His Word is what moves the heart of God. Asking is the activity of that faith!

We see this in Luke 4:25–27, where Jesus is unable to do miracles in Nazareth because of the people's unbelief. He says to those in the synagogue,

> But I tell you truly, many widows were in Israel in the days of Elijah, when the heaven was shut up three years and six months, and there was a great famine throughout all the land; but to none of them was Elijah sent except to Zarephath, in the region of Sidon, to a woman who was a widow. And many lepers were in Israel in the time of Elisha the prophet, and none of them was cleansed except Naaman the Syrian.

This Scripture helps us understand that God was not responding to great need. There were many lepers and many widows in those days Jesus mentioned, but only Naaman and the widow of Zarephath had their needs met. These were the ones who were willing to believe God.

If the Lord had simply responded to human need, everyone would have been ministered to. But He only responded to these two people. This is because the Lord responds to faith in the midst of need, not to need! When we ask God for something, we are moving in faith. This is why He can know before we ask, but only at the release of our faith through asking does He get involved.

Jesus tells us in Luke 11:13 that we must ask our heavenly Father for the Holy Spirit, who will then freely give us this good gift. Without question, we see that the Father gives the Holy

Spirit to those who *ask* Him. As we are thirsty for the Lord, may our faith be recognized through our asking. May we cry to the Lord and ask Him to endue us from above with the precious presence and power of the Holy Spirit.

## Actively Receiving and Speaking

As we ask for the Holy Spirit to fill us, we must also actively receive. The Holy Spirit will come into our spirit. This is what John 7:38 is declaring when it tells us that rivers will flow from the innermost part of our being. This is from the depths of our spirit. When the Holy Spirit comes into our lives at our invitation, He takes up residence in our spirit. As this occurs, the gift of tongues can begin to flow out of our spirit, into our mouth, and manifest from our lips.

We saw that this is what happened in Acts 2:4, but note that as the disciples were filled with the Holy Spirit, *they* "began to speak with other tongues as the Spirit gave them utterance." The Holy Spirit did not open their lips and move their tongues in their mouths. *They* did it. When the infilling of the Spirit touches us, we must by faith open our mouths and start making sounds and noises. This can be very intimidating, yet it is a simple response in faith to what is happening in the depths of our spirit. The power of the Holy Spirit will move through my mouth and yours in the form of tongues, but we must begin to speak. The word *utterance* in the Greek here is *apophtheggomai*. Part of its meaning is "to enunciate." This is the idea of forming words properly and releasing them in a clear sound. It is also the idea of pronouncing words correctly. These who were baptized in the Holy Spirit began to speak and enunciate under the influence and power of the Holy Spirit. They were the ones, however, who were doing the speaking.

This is so important because it can become a stumbling block to us actually experiencing and releasing the power of the sovereign Lord. I can want something to be of God so badly that I don't do my part in the matter. We have to do the speaking, as the Holy Spirit gives utterance. When we do, we can potentially unlock the dam that is in us and experience a flow of the Spirit through us that changes everything. The rivers of water deep in our spirit begin to flow out with supernatural purpose.

One other thing I want to mention here is that when we thirst, ask and receive the infilling and baptism of the Holy Spirit, as we begin to speak, we must be willing to allow unknown sounds to come out of our mouths. This is the intimidating part. As you or I begin to make sounds that are in an unknown language to us, it can seem strange and awkward. Yet this is the gift of tongues operating in us. We cannot evaluate what this gift may sound like in the natural.

Remember that potentially, we are speaking in the language of men and/or angels, as I mentioned in chapter 1. We also looked at the apostle Paul's mention of this phenomenon: "Though I speak with the tongues of men and of angels, but have not love, I have become sounding brass or a clanging cymbal" (1 Corinthians 13:1). The language that can come from our lips as we began to speak in tongues can be present-day languages from the earth, forgotten languages of times gone by from the earth, and also heavenly languages spoken by angels. I cannot therefore judge what the language I am speaking may sound like. I have to, by faith, bear witness to it in the Holy Spirit and trust that what I am receiving is from the Lord.

I think Jesus actually addressed this when He talked about asking the Father for the Holy Spirit. In Luke 11:11–13, He spoke of the loving Father, who only gives good gifts and will not give us something bad when we are believing Him and asking for something good:

> If a son asks for bread from any father among you, will he give him a stone? Or if he asks for a fish, will he give him a serpent instead of a fish? Or if he asks for an egg, will he offer him a scorpion? If you then, being evil, know how to give good gifts to your children, how much more will your heavenly Father give the Holy Spirit to those who ask Him!

The Father is not going to give us, or allow us to be given, something that is evil when we are believing Him for the goodness of the Holy Spirit. We must believe in the goodness of God as our Father, and that He would never allow this to occur. You and I can believe that the tongues we speak forth from our mouths at the time we are being baptized and immersed in the Spirit of God are good and are from God. No matter what they sound like, they are heaven's gift into our lives, and we can receive them as such, without question or debate. Our lives will change as a result, which will thrust us into a new arena and adventure from God!

*Four*

# THE FILLING
# OF THE SPIRIT

E ven though there is an initial baptism of the Holy Spirit that Jesus and others promised we could receive, many subsequent fillings can occur. These additional fillings can involve our speaking in tongues and engaging the Holy Spirit through this act. We see this in the experience of the disciples in the book of Acts. After their initial baptism with the Holy Spirit in Acts 2, other times are recorded when the disciples were filled again and again.

I want to make it abundantly clear that as those who are empowered through the baptism of the Holy Spirit, I believe we can pray in the spirit or in tongues at will. This is what Paul said in 1 Corinthians 14:15: "What is the conclusion then? I will pray with the spirit, and I will also pray with the understanding. I will sing with the spirit, and I will also sing with the under-standing." Notice that Paul said, "*I will*." He is declaring that praying, singing or speaking in tongues is a choice of our will, once we have received the baptism of the Holy Spirit.

I don't have to experience some special sense of the Lord's presence to operate in the gift of tongues. The Holy Spirit now dwells in me in this new dimension, and I can draw from Him at will. Just as I don't need to feel something special to speak in my natural language, neither do I need to feel something special to pray in the spirit or in tongues. I can will it to be so and experience the presence of the Lord as I minister to Him through tongues.

As we experience new fillings of the Spirit, however, tongues can also be part of these encounters. Once we are baptized in the Holy Spirit, tongues can become a primary release of the presence of the Holy Spirit in us and through us. Whether it is in everyday life where we are in constant communion with the Lord, or perhaps in an encounter where we are experiencing a dramatic time in His presence, tongues become part of these happenings.

Paul tells us in Ephesians 6:18 that we are to be "praying always with all prayer and supplication in the Spirit, being watchful to this end with all perseverance and supplication for all the saints." How can someone *pray always*? When we have tongues operating in our life as a result of the baptism of the Holy Spirit, it is possible. For me, whenever I am in a place of prayer, speaking in tongues is a big part of what I do as I commune with the Lord and seek His heart. But as I go about my day, regardless of what I do, I can be praying under my breath in tongues and no one knows it. This allows me to stay in constant communion with the Lord, all while taking care of my daily responsibilities. It keeps me connected and joined to Him, and it allows me to fulfill Scripture and be *watchful* in all things. I can have my guard up in the spirit world, yet take care of the business of life in the natural realm.

This is the power of tongues. This is part of being *filled with the Spirit*. Ephesians 5:18–20 exhorts us to be filled with the Spirit, along with giving us some insight into how:

> And do not be drunk with wine, in which is dissipation; but
> be filled with the Spirit, speaking to one another in psalms and
> hymns and spiritual songs, singing and making melody in your
> heart to the Lord, giving thanks always for all things to God
> the Father in the name of our Lord Jesus Christ.

Once I am baptized in the Holy Spirit, it is my responsibility
to stay filled! This is why we are admonished to "be filled with
the Spirit." We are to posture ourselves in such a way that the
fullness of the presence of God controls us.

## Walking in the Spirit

God's presence in us, filling and controlling us, is what it means
for us to walk in the Spirit. In Galatians 5:16, this is what Paul
urges us to do: "I say then: Walk in the Spirit, and you shall not
fulfill the lust of the flesh." Walking in the Spirit is another way
of declaring that we are filled with the Spirit. In other words,
we are allowing the Holy Spirit full control over us. Notice
that when we walk in and are filled with the Holy Spirit, we
do not fulfill the lust of the flesh. The flesh has no more pull
on us, because the Spirit is dominating and ruling our desires
and passions.

There is a divine connection for us between walking this way
and operating in tongues. Notice that in his exhortation, Paul
says we can speak to ourselves and to others through psalms,
hymns and *spiritual songs*. I take this to mean that we can sing
and worship in our natural language, but also in our prayer
language (whether it is an angelic tongue or an earthly one).
The wellspring of the Holy Spirit can flow through us in our
known human language, but also in the gift of tongues as we
worship in a language we do not know naturally. This language

can carry the very aroma of heaven, and it can permeate and change the atmosphere in every area of our life.

As we walk in and are filled with the Spirit through these places, we are also keeping ourselves in the love of God. In the book credited to him, Jude tells us of the power speaking in tongues has to keep us joined to God's love: "But you, beloved, building yourselves up on your most holy faith, praying in the Holy Spirit, keep yourselves in the love of God, looking for the mercy of our Lord Jesus Christ unto eternal life" (verses 20–21). When we pray in the Holy Spirit, which is a reference to tongues, we are keeping ourselves in the love of God. This means our life and perspective are being fashioned by God's love, rather than by the cruelties of the devil. The awareness of God's love is securing us and settling our fears. It also, however, is shaping our attitude toward others. This occurs because we are being filled with the Holy Spirit as we pray in tongues and exercise this realm.

Paul also said that as a result of being filled, we give thanks. First Corinthians 14:15–16 shows that when we pray in tongues, we can be giving thanks:

> What is the conclusion then? I will pray with the spirit, and I will also pray with the understanding. I will sing with the spirit, and I will also sing with the understanding. Otherwise, if you bless with the spirit, how will he who occupies the place of the uninformed say "Amen" at your giving of thanks, since he does not understand what you say?

Paul was making an effort to help the Corinthian church operate more efficiently in the Spirit. In the midst of this, he shows us that part of what tongues do is help us give thanks to God. (We will talk more about this in a later chapter.) Part of being filled with the Holy Spirit as we minister to the Lord in tongues is that it forms and releases a spirit of gratitude in us.

Releasing this gratitude in us is one of the greatest powers of our gift of tongues. We are able to say "thank You" to the Lord on a whole new level as we are filled with the Spirit of the living God. This gives us a new perspective to live life from. A thankful heart, released through tongues from the fullness of the Spirit, is so much better than a bitter and ungrateful spirit. Through the fullness of the Holy Spirit and the unleashing of the spiritual language of tongues, we express our appreciation to the Lord. Any acidic bitterness of soul is replaced with the sweetness of a heart formed by His presence. This is a result of being filled with the Spirit and honoring the Lord with and through the gift of tongues.

## Empowered in a Moment

The filling of the Holy Spirit unlocks the use of tongues. It is almost like a pressure valve on something that needs relief and release. When the fullness builds up in us, it needs to be expressed. This is quite often what tongues can do. As we are filled, the gift of tongues becomes a means of unleashing the marvelous fullness that overtakes us. We must learn to operate in the fullness of the Spirit on a daily basis and release that fullness through the gift of tongues.

*We must learn to operate in the fullness of the Spirit on a daily basis and release that fullness through the gift of tongues.*

There will be times beyond our everyday experience, however, when we also experience dramatic fillings of the Spirit. This happened to those in the early Church. They had all experienced an initial baptism in the Holy Spirit, with the manifestation of tongues. Many times, after that initial baptism, however, the Holy Spirit would come on them in a moment of time and empower them for that instance. These fillings would be accompanied by tongues and their operation. Let's look at some of the places where the early believers were empowered in such a moment.

In Acts 4, Peter was filled with the Spirit in such a moment. He was with John, and the two of them were being interrogated by the religious leaders of their day because a lame man had been healed. The leaders demanded of them, "By what power or by what name have you done this?" In reply, Peter was empowered to reply with great boldness because he was "filled with the Holy Spirit" (verses 7–8). As the two disciples were in what appeared to be a perilous position, the Holy Spirit filled Peter so that he powerfully responded to the leaders' questioning.

My supposition is that Peter's fullness and boldness of the Spirit flowed out of a heart that was already prepared as a result of his communing daily with the Spirit through the gift of tongues. If Peter had been living a carnal, natural life, would the Holy Spirit have had the power to fill him in such a way at that critical moment of time? I think not. But Peter had been walking in the Spirit and was already being filled on a daily basis. As a result, in this defining moment in front of the religious leaders, the Holy Spirit could fill him powerfully.

The gift of tongues keeps us in communion with the Spirit and prepares our hearts. Again, this is what 2 Corinthians 13:14 speaks of when it talks of the communion of the Holy Spirit: "The grace of the Lord Jesus Christ, and the love of God, and the communion of the Holy Spirit be with you all. Amen." Tongues are a means of walking in communion with the Spirit of God. This gift keeps that connection in place. The result is a prepared heart in the moment when we need it.

This is what happened with Peter and John in front of the intimidating religious leaders of Israel. Acts 4:13 gives us a glimpse of how the disciples' fullness and boldness amazed their challengers: "Now when they saw the boldness of Peter and John, and perceived that they were uneducated and untrained men, they marveled. And they realized that they had been with Jesus." Notice it was the boldness that amazed these leaders and caused them to marvel. This was a result of Peter having a prepared heart, which allowed the fullness of the Holy Spirit to come upon him. If we are to have moments like this, we must keep ourselves filled on a daily basis. Part of preparing our hearts comes through ministering to the Lord in tongues. We can then be positioned for moments of great empowerment in the Holy Spirit.

Acts 4:31 shows us another time when the Holy Spirit filled the disciples. This instance took place after Peter and John were released to return to their company of believers. They had been threatened, and their challengers had sought to make them afraid. As they returned to the other believers, they began to pray, with the result of being filled with the Spirit again: "And when they had prayed, the place where they were assembled together was shaken; and they were all filled with the Holy Spirit, and they spoke the word of God with boldness."

The weight of God's presence caused a physical shaking, and a filling with the Holy Spirit produced boldness in them to speak and declare the word. I am sure part of their praying was in tongues. Once you have been baptized in the Spirit and learn to operate in the gift of tongues, it becomes a normal part of your spiritual operation. As the disciples prayed, I am sure it was both in their natural language and also in the cry of the Holy Spirit through them in tongues. This resulted in the fresh filling.

One of the main attributes of the Holy Spirit is to empower us in prayer. Romans 8:26 says that in our weakness, we are strengthened for effective prayer: "Likewise the Spirit also helps in our weaknesses. For we do not know what we should pray for as we ought, but the Spirit Himself makes intercession for us with groanings which cannot be uttered." At least part of this help we receive is through praying in the gift of tongues, which flows through us as a perfect prayer born out of the passion of the Holy Spirit. This is one of the things that makes tongues so powerful. These groanings the verse mentions can flow through us. We are then taken out of the natural realm of prayer and propelled into the supernatural place. This allows things to move in the unseen spiritual realm, which alters things in the natural realm.

This is what was happening in the prayer meeting we just read about. The disciples' cry in the midst of the threats against them was filled with the supernatural realm of the Spirit. This would have involved the gift of tongues and its operation. Tongues press us past our weakness in prayer and make us powerful before God. The result is an empowerment coming to us that overcomes any fear and moves us into new places of function and power.

> *Tongues press us past our weakness in prayer and make us powerful before God.*

Acts 13:8–11 is yet another place where we see the disciples filled again with the Spirit. Paul is dealing with Elymas the sorcerer at the same time that he is seeking to win a certain leader to the Lord:

> But Elymas the sorcerer (for so his name is translated) withstood them, seeking to turn the proconsul away from the faith. Then Saul, who also is called Paul, filled with the Holy Spirit,

looked intently at him and said, "O full of all deceit and all fraud, you son of the devil, you enemy of all righteousness, will you not cease perverting the straight ways of the Lord? And now, indeed, the hand of the Lord is upon you, and you shall be blind, not seeing the sun for a time."

And immediately a dark mist fell on him, and he went around seeking someone to lead him by the hand.

As Paul was filled with the Holy Spirit, he spoke judgment on that which was resisting the purposes of God. Again, this kind of fullness of the Spirit would have had tongues involved. Paul would have kept himself built up and strengthened in the Spirit through his perpetual practice of speaking in tongues. We know this because of what he said in 1 Corinthians 14:18: "I thank my God I speak with tongues more than you all." Paul claimed to practice speaking in tongues more than the whole Corinthian church. So when he stood and confronted this devilish sorcerer, it was out of the empowerment of tongues operating in his life. The Holy Spirit could fill and strengthen him so that he was operating in a judicial place in the spirit world and could establish judgment against that which was resisting God. The private preparation in Paul's life through the practice of speaking in tongues empowered him in this public moment. Here we again see the connection between tongues, the fullness of the Spirit and operating in the power of God.

## Our Walk Affects Others

It is important to realize that the fullness of the Holy Spirit we walk in will affect the people around us. Look at Acts 13:50–52, still another place where the disciples were filled again with the Spirit. This passage shows persecution and resistance being brought against Paul and Barnabas and their apostolic ministry.

In response, they obey the word of Jesus and render judgment against the city of Antioch, which will not receive them:

> But the Jews stirred up the devout and prominent women and the chief men of the city, raised up persecution against Paul and Barnabas, and expelled them from their region. But they shook off the dust from their feet against them, and came to Iconium. And the disciples were filled with joy and with the Holy Spirit.

Jesus had told His apostles in Luke 9:5 that should a city reject them, they should render judgment against it and move on to the next place: "And whoever will not receive you, when you go out of that city, shake off the very dust from your feet as a testimony against them." This is what Paul and Barnabas are doing. When an apostolic leader does this under the leading of the Holy Spirit, a city can forfeit the move of God and the purpose of God within it until it repents.

After Paul and Barnabas do this at Antioch, they go on to Iconium, where even more disciples are filled with joy and the Holy Spirit. Because Paul and Barnabas are filled, these disciples become filled as well. This is why we should practice praying in tongues regularly. The fullness of the Spirit that this gift produces in us should cause others to be filled, too.

The truth is that who and what we are will affect others. When Peter and John encountered the lame man at the Gate Beautiful in Acts 3:6–8, Peter "gave" the man what he had:

> Then Peter said, "Silver and gold I do not have, but what I do have I give you: In the name of Jesus Christ of Nazareth, rise up and walk." And he took him by the right hand and lifted him up, and immediately his feet and ankle bones received strength. So he, leaping up, stood and walked and entered the temple with them—walking, leaping, and praising God.

As Peter took of the fullness of what he was walking in and gave it away, the man was healed. This is another reason it is so imperative that we stay filled with the Holy Spirit. As we walk in His fullness, we are then ready for any such moments that we might encounter.

I think this is what Paul might have been encouraging Timothy to do in 2 Timothy 4:2: "Preach the word! Be ready in season and out of season. Convince, rebuke, exhort, with all longsuffering and teaching." Being ready in season and out of season speaks of walking in such a way that when something is expected of me, I am prepared, but when something is a surprise, I am equally as well prepared. No matter what might be happening, I am filled with the Holy Spirit and am ready to release His fullness to others.

Praying in tongues is one of the ways that we can keep ourselves and our hearts in a constantly prepared state. Again, it is not that we are spending hours and hours a day in prayer. We know that real life would not allow that. But we can pray as we go. The gift of tongues and its operation will allow this. As we perfect this practice, we can be ready in season and out. We can live a life of fullness that touches others and makes them full as well. Paul and Barnabas brought the fullness

*Being ready in season and out of season speaks of walking in such a way that when something is expected of me, I am prepared, but when something is a surprise, I am equally as well prepared.*

of the Holy Spirit to those in Iconium because they themselves were filled. As we seek the Lord and use the gift of tongues, it can help us walk in the same way they did. Every day can be an adventure as we walk before the Lord!

# *Five*

# NEW TONGUES

Several phrases in Scripture imply speaking in tongues. Consider the phrases Paul uses in 1 Corinthians 14:15: "What is the conclusion then? I will *pray with the spirit*, and I will also pray with the understanding. I will *sing with the spirit*, and I will also sing with the understanding" (emphasis added). This whole chapter of Scripture speaks about the use of spiritual gifts in the Corinthian church. In talking about praying with the spirit and singing with the spirit, Paul is referring to tongues, and he is seeking to help the Corinthian believers understand how to use them.

The whole phrase *with the spirit* is actually one Greek word, *pneuma*, which means "a current of air" or "a breath blast." Paul is endeavoring to help these believers understand that the Holy Spirit is like the wind. Jesus acknowledged this is John 3:8: "The wind blows where it wishes, and you hear the sound of it, but cannot tell where it comes from and where it goes. So is everyone who is born of the Spirit." At times, a person under the influence of the Spirit of the Lord may seem erratic to others. This does not give us license to be irresponsible, yet when we follow the leading of the Holy Spirit, we may at times make decisions that seem illogical. They will bear out as the wisdom of the Lord, however, if we are truly following Him.

Jesus said that no one tells the Holy Spirit what to do; He is like the wind that blows where He wishes. People feel the effects and hear the sound, but they cannot control the wind. They simply have to get into agreement with Him. If the Holy Spirit is leading us to do something, we do not have to understand it logically or make sense of it. When it is coming from God's insight into a situation, it will prove itself correct. This is the *pneuma* of God moving us wherever He desires. The English translation of 1 Corinthians 14 phrases part of this process in us as praying and singing *with the spirit*, which implies that we cooperate and agree with what we sense the Holy Spirit is doing.

As we pray and sing with the spirit, we can release the *pneuma* of God through the gift of tongues. Through tongues, we unlock the breath and current of air that resides in us. We come into cooperation with the wind of the Holy Spirit as we pray in the spirit and/or speak in tongues. In the process, we learn to follow the dictates of what we sense in our inner man.

*We come into cooperation with the wind of the Holy Spirit as we pray in the spirit and/or speak in tongues.*

Paul displayed this in Colossians 1:29, when he spoke of moving in agreement with what was happening inside him: "To this end I also labor, striving according to His working which works in me mightily." Paul's labors were connected to the working of the Lord, which was working mightily in him. Paul was not trying to create something out of his own power and energy. He was allowing the impetus of the Holy Spirit inside him to move and motivate him. When we are walking full of the Holy Spirit, we will be driven from the inside out. This is what the gift of tongues actually is. We begin to pray in and from our spirit, which unleashes the unction of the Lord from the inside out.

The great healing revivalist Smith Wigglesworth is purported to have said, "If the Spirit doesn't move me, then I move the Spirit." He had discovered that the Holy Spirit who lived inside him could be stirred up. This is what Paul exhorts Timothy to do in 2 Timothy 1:6: "Therefore I remind you to stir up the gift of God which is in you through the laying on of my hands." Paul was pressing Timothy not to allow the gifting to lie dormant in him. The word *stir* in the Greek here is *anazopureo*. It means "to rekindle," but also "to ignite a fire," and one of its root words implies a "live beast." Paul was telling Timothy to stir up the fire and not let it go out. He also was letting him know there was a living, powerful force inside him—even a beast. Paul was saying to Timothy, "Unleash the Beast!" This was the gift of God. This was tongues. When we know how to move in this gift of a prayer language, it stirs up all that is in us. We will be praying and perhaps singing with the spirit. We are in concert with the very power of God that lives in us.

Another term that can be used to communicate the gift of tongues is *groaning*. Romans 8:26 says that the Holy Spirit creates groanings that are actually intercession with us and for us: "Likewise the Spirit also helps in our weaknesses. For we do not know what we should pray for as we ought, but the Spirit Himself makes intercession for us with groanings which cannot be uttered." Groanings can be more than tongues, but definitely can involve tongues. We know this because Paul explains what he is speaking of as something that cannot be uttered. In other words, there was no natural language that could adequately communicate his prayers. This would mean it was an unlearned language of heavenly origin.

This is one of the things tongues are for. They give us the ability to say things in the spirit world that we otherwise could not communicate. I have heard many testimonies of people who were actually filled with the Holy Spirit because they were frustrated at the inability they felt to tell God how much they loved Him. There was a passion inside them that they could not express adequately. In the midst of this, the Lord would graciously baptize them in the Holy Spirit, and they would find themselves speaking in a language they had never learned. The lack of fulfillment they had felt so deeply in seeking to express their heart to the Lord was instantly satisfied because of the tongues flowing from their heart out of their lips. This kind of tongue can be included in those "groanings which cannot be uttered."

## Tongues as a Sign

There is then the phrase *new tongues*, which is used to describe the experience of this gift as a sign. In Mark 16:17–18, as Mark is recording what Jesus said about the power and gifting that we as believers are to walk in, this term *new tongues* is placed in the list:

> And these signs will follow those who believe: In My name they will cast out demons; they will speak with new tongues; they will take up serpents; and if they drink anything deadly, it will by no means hurt them; they will lay hands on the sick, and they will recover.

The list includes healing, deliverance and divine protection, yet these *new tongues* are listed as well, included as one of the signs that we believers will walk in. The word *signs* is the Greek word *semeion*, meaning "an indication," especially supernaturally. The signs listed here are indications to others that we belong to Jesus and are authorized to represent Him. This is the reason for the signs.

Hebrews 2:3–4 give us further insight into how these signs are used to convince people that we are sent as God's representatives:

> How shall we escape if we neglect so great a salvation, which at the first began to be spoken by the Lord, and was confirmed to us by those who heard Him, God also bearing witness both with signs and wonders, with various miracles, and gifts of the Holy Spirit, according to His own will?

These signs are supposed to be so substantial that if people reject them, there are serious consequences. This passage actually mentions four distinct things that bear witness that someone has been sent from the Lord: *signs, wonders, miracles* and *gifts of the Holy Spirit*. These can overlap with each other, but they are clearly given to help people accept and believe another person who is carrying a message God wants them to hear.

## Marked by God

As we look at these four things that bear witness to God's representatives, let's first consider *signs* more deeply. We have already seen that this word in the Greek means "an indication." We see God using signs to mark His representatives in the Old Testament, as well as in the New Testament. Exodus 4:1–9 shows that God gave Moses three signs to demonstrate to the people of God that He had appeared to him. As the Lord was sending Moses back to deliver the children of Israel from their Egyptian bondage, Moses expressed deep concern that the people would not believe God had sent him. God therefore gave Moses three different signs to attest to the fact that he had encountered Him:

> Then Moses answered and said, "But suppose they will not believe me or listen to my voice; suppose they say, 'The Lord has not appeared to you.'"
>
> So the Lord said to him, "What is that in your hand?"
>
> He said, "A rod."
>
> And He said, "Cast it on the ground." So he cast it on the ground, and it became a serpent; and Moses fled from it. Then the Lord said to Moses, "Reach out your hand and take it by the tail" (and he reached out his hand and caught it, and it became a rod in his hand), "that they may believe that the Lord God of their fathers, the God of Abraham, the God of Isaac, and the God of Jacob, has appeared to you."
>
> Furthermore the Lord said to him, "Now put your hand in your bosom." And he put his hand in his bosom, and when he took it out, behold, his hand was leprous, like snow. And He said, "Put your hand in your bosom again." So he put his hand in his bosom again, and drew it out of his bosom, and behold, it was restored like his other flesh. "Then it will be, if they do not believe you, nor heed the message of the first sign, that they may believe the message of the latter sign. And it shall be, if they do not believe even these two signs, or listen to your voice, that you shall take water from the river and pour it on the dry land. The water which you take from the river will become blood on the dry land."

God gave Moses these three signs to convince the children of Israel that He had indeed appeared to him. The word *sign* in the Hebrew in these verses is the word *owth*, which means "a signal, a flag, beacon, monument" and a "mark" or "evidence." So something supernatural being manifested is God waving a flag. It is God flashing a beacon. It is God raising a monument and giving evidence that this is from Him. To reject this is to reject the Lord Himself.

We as God's people are to carry signs as a mark that we have been sent from the Lord. These three things that God gave Moses speak of significant issues. The rod becoming a snake, then turning back into a rod, revealed a couple of things. First, rods speak of authority. We must realize that in every place of authority, there is a serpent. In other words, unless we are in submission to the Lord and are walking in fear of Him, we will abuse authority. God was revealing this to Moses, who needed to know that there was a potential snake in the rod God was about to put into his hand. As Moses wielded this rod, he had to do so under the authority of God Himself. When Moses was told to pick the rod back up by the tail, it was because he was to grab the *small end*. As we carry the authority of God, we operate together with Him. But we must always realize that we carry the *small end*.

> *We as God's people are to carry signs as a mark that we have been sent from the Lord.*

According to 2 Corinthians 4:7, "We have this treasure in earthen vessels, that the excellence of the power may be of God and not of us." Notice that the awareness of who we are as earthen vessels causes us to be mindful that the power belongs to God and not to us. We have a part to play, but it is God's power in and through us that does the work. We simply learn how to use what operates in us, whereas God is the source. This is what the Lord wanted Moses to know, so that he would not misuse what God had placed in His hand.

The second sign was God healing leprosy. He instructed Moses to place his hand inside his clothing, and then take it out again. The hand became leprous, and when Lord told him to place it back into his bosom a second time, it was healed. This was the Lord demonstrating His power to heal both physically and spiritually. Leprosy is a physical disease that Jesus healed many people of during His earthly ministry. It also speaks, however, of the spiritual condition of sin, because leprosy makes people "unclean." If a priest found them leprous, they were isolated and had to cry out, *"Unclean! Unclean!"* if others came near. The leprosy not only ended up destroying them physically; it also separated them from family, friends and loved ones. Further, it eventually brought them death through horrible means. This is what sin does. Undealt with, sin will bring us spiritual death.

James 1:14–15 shows the process sin takes to bring us death both spiritually and physically: "But each one is tempted when he is drawn away by his own desires and enticed. Then, when desire has conceived, it gives birth to sin; and sin, when it is full-grown, brings forth death." Notice that death is not immediate; it is the end of the process. This is what deceives people. They enter into sin, and nothing bad seems to happen. But the process of dying has started.

Satan deceived Eve with this concept. In his conversation with her in Genesis 3:2–5, he posed the question of whether she would really die if she ate of the fruit, as God had said:

> And the woman said to the serpent, "We may eat the fruit of the trees of the garden; but of the fruit of the tree which is in the midst of the garden, God has said, 'You shall not eat it, nor shall you touch it, lest you die.'"
>
> Then the serpent said to the woman, "You will not surely die. For God knows that in the day you eat of it your eyes will be opened, and you will be like God, knowing good and evil."

Notice how Satan said to Eve, "You will not surely die." We know that Eve ate of the fruit. To her amazement, *she didn't die.* We know this is true because she then convinced Adam to eat it. After all, she had not died physically. The problem was that the dying process had started.

Death is not just about our physical being ceasing to breathe. It is about separation from God. Revelation 21:8 refers to the second death: "But the cowardly, unbelieving, abominable, murderers, sexually immoral, sorcerers, idolaters, and all liars shall have their part in the lake which burns with fire and brimstone, which is the second death." My point is that death is a complete and total separation from God. The real dying is not physical; it is spiritual. Physical death is the *first death*. Separation from God in eternal judgment is the *second death*. So when Moses put his hand in his bosom and brought it back out leprous, then did it again and brought it out clean, this was a demonstration of God's healing power physically and spiritually. This was a sign that God had indeed appeared to Moses and had sent him to deliver the people.

The third sign was that Moses was to pour river water on dry land and it would become blood. The Nile River was considered a god, as were some of the fish in it. When the river turned to blood, this was a display of God's judgment against the gods of Egypt. It could even have been a prophetic declaration that the blood of the coming Messiah would judge all other gods. Regardless, this action on Moses' part would serve as a sign that God had sent him, and that the Lord was greater than the gods of Egypt, where His people were held captive. These three signs were designed to attest to the One whom Moses was representing—the Lord Himself.

## Wonders That Speak

Hebrews 2:3–4 also mentions *wonders* that will speak of and give credibility to the representatives whom God has sent. In the

Greek, the word *wonder* is *teras*, meaning "a prodigy or omen." An omen is something that seems prophetic in nature. It is speaking of and revealing something yet to come, and it can be predictive. Sometimes supernatural things are not just about what happens; they are about the message connected to the events.

For instance, many of the wonders Jesus performed were not just about the things that happened, but about the message connected to them. These wonders reveal something about God—the way He does things and what is to come. When Jesus turned the water into wine in John 2:1–11, the people at the feast were blessed. Jesus' disciples were also greatly encouraged as they began to believe who Jesus really was. This wonderful occurrence, however, has also spoken prophetically to us throughout the generations that have passed since its actual occurrence. To get the full effect of this, let's look at the scriptural chronicle of this event:

> On the third day there was a wedding in Cana of Galilee, and the mother of Jesus was there. Now both Jesus and His disciples were invited to the wedding. And when they ran out of wine, the mother of Jesus said to Him, "They have no wine."
>
> Jesus said to her, "Woman, what does your concern have to do with Me? My hour has not yet come."
>
> His mother said to the servants, "Whatever He says to you, do it."
>
> Now there were set there six waterpots of stone, according to the manner of purification of the Jews, containing twenty or thirty gallons apiece. Jesus said to them, "Fill the waterpots with water." And they filled them up to the brim. And He said to them, "Draw some out now, and take it to the master of the feast." And they took it. When the master of the feast had tasted the water that was made wine, and did not know where it came from (but the servants who had drawn the water knew), the master of the feast called the bridegroom. And he said to

him, "Every man at the beginning sets out the good wine, and when the guests have well drunk, then the inferior. You have kept the good wine until now!"

This beginning of signs Jesus did in Cana of Galilee, and manifested His glory; and His disciples believed in Him.

We can see so many *prophetic omens* in this one event. For instance, this happened on the *third day*. The third day is the day of resurrection. Many have preached, and rightfully so, that God will bring us through our time in the grave, into a time of His resurrection life and power—a demonstration of who He is in us and through us. Still others have emphasized that this wondrous event took place at a wedding. They have declared that God desires to bring us into covenant relationship with Him and His people. As we come into this place of deep connection, the water of our experience will become the wine of His presence and life.

Several other prophetic omens can be seen in this account as well. The biggest one would be that God is *saving the best for last*. This is what the master of the feast declared—that the best wine was saved for last. This has been a prophetic cry throughout the Church Age. What God will do before the Second Coming of the Lord will far surpass anything that has been done previously. This message is clearly wrapped up in this story of Jesus' first wonder, which has predictive essence in it. It was an omen of that which is yet to come.

> *Many times, when God does wonders, it is as much about the message connected to a wonder as it is about the event itself.*

Many times, when God does wonders, it is as much about the message connected to a wonder as it is about the event itself. This is why we as believers must always ask what God is saying through something supernatural that occurs. If we do not ask this, we potentially can miss the main effect of what the Lord is showing us.

## Explosive Miracles

Another thing Hebrews 2:4 mentions is *various miracles*. The word *miracles* in the Greek is *dunamis*. It means "a force, miraculous power or ability." From *dunamis* we get the word *dynamite*. A miracle can be an explosive thing that gets people's attention. God uses miracles to display who He is and quite often His heart toward us. He loves us greatly. Miracles can be a confirming sign of this. There is nothing like having God demonstrate His care for us through His miracle-working power on our behalf.

I want to relate a couple of stories that illustrate this. A few years ago, we were holding a special healing service in a small rural town with a population of perhaps a few thousand people. The word had been spread around town that there would be a healing service and that anyone sick, diseased or in need should come. A man attended who been smitten with a debilitating stroke just a few days before this meeting. The illness had left his speech slurred and his body basically immobile. His friends had actually carried him into the meeting and had set him on a chair, and two of them sat on either side of him to hold him upright. Otherwise, he would have fallen out of his chair in his paralyzed state.

The interesting thing about this meeting was that as I had prayed concerning it, I felt I had heard the Lord say there would be *notable miracles*. This was very intriguing. We had seen some really good things happen, but *notable miracles* were another dimension. This comes from Acts 4:16, where the religious leaders of the day were struggling with what to do with Peter and John after the healing of the lame man at the Gate Beautiful. The leaders asked, "What shall we do to these men? For, indeed, that a *notable miracle* has been done through them is evident to all who dwell in Jerusalem, and we cannot deny it" (emphasis added).

A notable miracle is one that cannot be denied. It demands a decision. It will not allow someone to stay neutral. In response to it, people have to decide what they will do with the claim of Jesus on their lives. I felt I had heard the Lord say that this kind of miracle would happen in this meeting. As the meeting progressed, a time came when the strong presence of the Lord was there. Luke 5:17 speaks of this also happening when Jesus was ministering:

> Now it happened on a certain day, as He was teaching, that there were Pharisees and teachers of the law sitting by, who had come out of every town of Galilee, Judea, and Jerusalem. And the power of the Lord was present to heal them.

The power of the Lord being present to heal is quite significant. This implies that God is near and desires to touch people in a miraculous way. I remember that we were singing the children's hymn "Jesus Loves Me" when His presence seemed to permeate the atmosphere. We were singing, "Jesus loves me, this I know, for the Bible tells me so. Little ones to Him belong; they are weak, but He is strong. Yes, Jesus loves me! Yes, Jesus loves me! Yes, Jesus loves me! The Bible tells me so." Such a simple, yet precious declaration of faith in the loving care of the Lord!

God's presence came close to us in that moment. As it did, we began by faith to pray and believe God for healing. A person from one of the healing teams went over to minister to this man. In that atmosphere charged with God's powerful presence, the man struggled in faith to stand up from his chair. The power of the Lord went through his body, completely eradicating and removing every effect of his stroke!

The first time I saw this man was when he came onto the platform to tell people what God had done. Remember, this was a small rural town, and many in the meeting knew about his illness, so they knew they were witnessing a bona fide miracle. It was not long before the whole town knew about it. They even broadcasted the miracle on their local radio station. The goodness and kindness of the Lord had been revealed, and through this notable miracle the whole town had seen a true witness of who the Lord is. Many in this little town tended to be quite religious, meaning they had allowed their religion to reduce God down to what He *used to do*. But here was a living demonstration of our God who still does miracles today. This whole town was given a witness to the Lord that is still there to this day.

The other miracle took place in the church I led. We regularly held healing services the first Saturday of every month. These were exciting and powerful times when we presented ourselves before the Lord and asked that He be glorified. There were always healings and miracles in these times. One miracle involved a young lady who had been a passenger in a car that was involved in an accident. This accident had happened while she and her friends were involved in doing something that they should not have been doing. She had spent some time in the hospital, but she had been discharged on crutches. She then attended a healing service, where again the power of the Lord was present to heal. People began to be healed in the auditorium as His presence moved. Those who were healed came onto the platform to share what God had done for them in His goodness.

As I turned at one point to see who was ready to share next, it was this young lady. She came onto the platform without any crutches, and she began to walk and then to run, demonstrating her complete and total healing. God had mended her in an instant. She then began to weep, not just because she was healed, but also because God's love was made manifest to her through His forgiveness. Remember, she had been injured while doing something she should not have done. Yet in His great love, God had healed and restored her, and in the process she knew that He had also forgiven her.

James 5:14–15 reveals that the same grace that brings healing also releases forgiveness:

> Is anyone among you sick? Let him call for the elders of the church, and let them pray over him, anointing him with oil in the name of the Lord. And the prayer of faith will save the sick, and the Lord will raise him up. And if he has committed sins, he will be forgiven.

Notice that God raises up the sick, but also simultaneously forgives their sins. This is a manifestation of His kindness and goodness. Psalm 103:1–3 also shows this aspect of God's kindness. He heals diseases, but also forgives sins and iniquities:

> Bless the LORD, O my soul; and all that is within me, bless His holy name! Bless the LORD, O my soul, and forget not all His benefits: who forgives all your iniquities, who heals all your diseases.

The forgiveness of sin and the healing of all infirmities are benefits of serving the Lord. They happen when His miraculous power is released. The miracles that take place are a physical declaration of God's unseen heart toward us. They show who He is in His kindness, goodness, generosity and liberality.

Miracles are a demonstration of God's Kingdom heart and passion toward us. This is why Jesus tells His disciples in Luke 10:8–9 that they should declare that the Kingdom of God is present when the sick are healed: "Whatever city you enter, and they receive you, eat such things as are set before you. And heal the sick there, and say to them, 'The kingdom of God has come near to you.'" Miracles and healings are physical depictions of unseen spiritual realities. As things are reset in the spirit world through the anointing and presence of who Jesus is, miracles, healings, signs and wonders are the result. His government, which is His Kingdom, becomes the ruling force rather than the powers of Satan. The consequence is that heaven comes into the earthly realm, and the goodness of God is revealed through these phenomena.

## Gifts Move through Our Soul

The last thing Hebrews 2:4 mentions is the *gifts of the Holy Spirit*. This phrase contains the interesting word *gifts*, which normally has something to do with grace. In this phrase, however, the word *gifts* is the Greek word *merismos*, which means "a separation or distribution." This word is the same one used in Hebrews 4:12 for *division*: "For the word of God is living and powerful, and sharper than any two-edged sword, piercing even to the division of soul and spirit, and of joints and marrow, and is a discerner of the thoughts and intents of the heart." The word *division* is this same word *merismos*. Several have taught that we need to discern what is soul and what is spirit, and they have implied or even taught that spirit is good and soul is bad. This is erroneous teaching and is not what this verse emphasizes. The soul is only negative in an unredeemed state. If the soul is renewed, however, it becomes a great asset to facilitate that which is flowing from the Holy Spirit of God within our spirit.

It is helpful to realize that when we were born again, our spirit was saved or came alive in God. It happened; it is done. My soul, however, is presently being saved, or is being renewed into the image of the One who created it. My body will be redeemed at the coming of the Lord Jesus and the resurrection from the dead. We are told that the living Word of God presently is piercing or skewering our soul and spirit together. This connected soul and spirit then have the ability to facilitate and release the gifting of the Holy Spirit. The Holy Spirit dwells within our spirit. For the gifting of the Spirit to be revealed and manifested through us, it must move through our soul, which consists of our mind, will and emotions.

When what the Holy Spirit is producing in us moves through our soul, this can involve our own personality, mindset and belief systems. If these are warped or wounded, then what is of the Holy Spirit can become tainted before it manifests through us. What starts as pure in our spirit can become defiled before it is distributed through us. If, however, we have been through the healing and restoring work of God in our soul, then a pure stream can flow through us. This is why we are told that God uses the distribution of the Holy Spirit's gifts through us to attest to Him and His desires.

Many different giftings of the Holy Spirit can potentially be distributed through us. One of those is tongues. Through the fullness/baptism of the Holy Spirit, I now have an ability to pray and speak in the gift of tongues, which is part of the language of the Holy Spirit within me. As the Spirit of God prays through me, it is facilitated through my soul. It can come out of my mouth in the form of tongues, which are the result of the unction of the Holy Spirit moving in my spirit, through my soul and out of my mouth. Without my spirit and soul being skewered together, there would be no means for the language of the Holy Spirit to come forth.

## The *New* in New Tongues

Jesus gives us demonstrations of the Holy Spirit such as tongues to prove that He sent us. *New tongues* is the phrase used to describe this sign in Mark 16:17. The word *new* is the Greek word *kainos*. It is a reference to something being *fresh*. This instance of the word *new* is not connected to age, but rather to freshness. Freshness is that which is life-giving and full of the unction of God. First John 2:7–8 gives us a further idea of how this word *new* is used:

> Brethren, I write no new commandment to you, but an old commandment which you have had from the beginning. The old commandment is the word which you heard from the beginning. Again, a new commandment I write to you, which thing is true in Him and in you, because the darkness is passing away, and the true light is already shining.

John uses this word *kainos* here, which is translated "new," concerning a command he is giving the followers of Jesus. First of all, John says, he is giving no *new* command, but an *old* one. Then he also says he is giving a *new* one. Not *new* in the sense of never having been heard before, but *new* in the sense of the freshness of the Holy Spirit being breathed upon it. The Holy Spirit was putting fresh, new life and emphasis on something the hearers already knew, and He was making it *new* and impacting.

As we have seen, Scripture also uses the word *new* in reference to the *new tongues* given to believers. This may not mean that such tongues were never heard before, although that could be the case. Regardless of whether or not such tongues are *new* in the sense of never being known, they are *new* in the sense of the power and life associated with them. When you speak in these tongues, they are like a river of living water flowing from you. Again, this is what Jesus said in John 7:37–39:

> On the last day, that great day of the feast, Jesus stood and cried out, saying, "If anyone thirsts, let him come to Me and drink. He who believes in Me, as the Scripture has said, out of his heart will flow rivers of living water." But this He spoke concerning the Spirit, whom those believing in Him would receive; for the Holy Spirit was not yet given, because Jesus was not yet glorified.

These new tongues are so powerful that they are like rivers flowing from the depths of our heart with power and might. They are renewing us and forcibly removing all hindrance in our spirit and soul out of the way. They are new tongues full of the life of God.

*New tongues* can also be joined to what the apostle Paul said in 1 Corinthians 12:7–10. Listing the different manifestations of the Holy Spirit that can be facilitated through our soul, he speaks of *different kinds of tongues*:

> But the manifestation of the Spirit is given to each one for the profit of all. for to one is given the word of wisdom through the Spirit, to another the word of knowledge through the same Spirit, to another faith by the same Spirit, to another gifts of healings by the same Spirit, to another the working of miracles, to another prophecy, to another discerning of spirits, to another different kinds of tongues, to another the interpretation of tongues.

When you receive tongues at the baptism and filling of the Holy Spirit, you receive a *prayer language*. (We will talk more of this in chapter 7.) Even though your prayer language might usually seem the same, there are times when the dialect or the sound of it changes. This can be the *new tongues* spoken of here. The Holy Spirit may begin to flow through you in a different way, for a different purpose. Perhaps it is just to bring freshness to you through a different release. It can, however, be *to do something different* in the spirit world.

> *Different tongues can have different impacts in the spirit realm. . . . Every voice and every sound has significance.*

Different tongues can have different impacts in the spirit realm. Paul says in 1 Corinthians 14:9–10 that every voice and every sound has significance:

> So likewise you, unless you utter by the tongue words easy to understand, how will it be known what is spoken? For you will be speaking into the air. There are, it may be, so many kinds of languages in the world, and none of them is without significance.

The word *languages* in this passage is the Greek word *phōnē*, and its root word carries the meaning of "a disclosure and/or a tone." Every tone or revelation/disclosure has significance, so the *tone* in a gift of tongues can be releasing new words of revelation and shifting things in that place. It can bring order to what is chaotic. It can bring placement to what is out of joint. This can occur through the Holy Spirit releasing *new tongues* through us.

We simply need to allow the outworking of the Holy Spirit to flow through us. We do not have to know what is occurring. Through faith, we simply allow the Holy Spirit to flow out of our spirit, through our soul, and we release sounds and languages of significance. Perhaps great alterations are occurring in the spirit realm that will manifest in the natural world. We may never fully know this side of heaven, yet maybe God has even allowed us to partner with Him in changing life on the planet!

*Six*

# A SIGN TO UNBELIEVERS

In the previous chapter, we spoke about how God uses signs and other things to reveal Himself to people and cultures. The Lord desires all to be saved and none to be lost. Scripture is full of this concept, and 2 Peter 3:9 clearly declares God's heart about it: "The Lord is not slack concerning His promise, as some count slackness, but is longsuffering toward us, not willing that any should perish but that all should come to repentance." This verse basically tells us not to allow the idea that nothing has happened yet to convince us that God does not care. Do not allow the fact that the Lord has not yet called things into judgment make you think that He is not really committed to holiness. Peter is saying the reason why there is no judgment yet is because God does not want any to perish. He desires all to be saved.

Even though God's heart is that everyone should be saved, not everyone will be. There are those who will resist God until the end. There will be no mercy or grace for such people, even though God's passion is for all to come to repentance. We must never allow the long-suffering of God to convince us that there will be no judgment. Yet because He wants everyone to be saved, He is working greatly to bring unbelievers to Himself.

*Even the gift of tongues is meant to convince unbelievers that God is real and that they should surrender their hearts to Him.*

Even the gift of tongues is meant to convince unbelievers that God is real and that they should surrender their hearts to Him.

This is what Paul addressed in 1 Corinthians 14:21–27, which shows that when tongues are operating properly, God will use them to convince unbelievers of their need for the Lord:

> In the law it is written:
> "With men of other tongues and other lips
> I will speak to this people;
> And yet, for all that, they will not hear Me,"
> says the Lord.
>
> Therefore tongues are for a sign, not to those who believe but to unbelievers; but prophesying is not for unbelievers but for those who believe. Therefore if the whole church comes together in one place, and all speak with tongues, and there come in those who are uninformed or unbelievers, will they not say that you are out of your mind? But if all prophesy, and an unbeliever or an uninformed person comes in, he is convinced by all, he is convicted by all. And thus the secrets of his heart are revealed; and so, falling down on his face, he will worship God and report that God is truly among you.
>
> How is it then, brethren? Whenever you come together, each of you has a psalm, has a teaching, has a tongue, has a revelation, has an interpretation. Let all things be done for edification. If anyone speaks in a tongue, let there be two or at the most three, each in turn, and let one interpret.

At first glance, it looks as if some of these verses conflict with each other. We are told that tongues are a sign to the unbeliever. Then we are told that if unbelievers come into a church setting and hear people speaking in tongues, they will say everyone is crazy. We have to take these statements in the context in which Paul made them. Note that Paul lists three different categories of people in these verses: *believers*, *unbelievers* and *the unlearned*. These are the three groups of people who can be impacted by the moving of the Holy Spirit and even the gift of tongues. Let's examine these groups a little more closely.

## Believers Quick to Believe

The *believers* are those who have set their faith in Jesus as Lord and Savior. More than that, they are the ones who tend to be open to the move of God and the way the Lord does things. They hunger for the Holy Spirit's operation and involvement in their lives. They are those who believe God quickly, just as Abraham did in Genesis 15:5–6, when God showed him the stars of the sky and promised that his descendants would be like those stars in number:

> Then He brought him outside and said, "Look now toward heaven, and count the stars if you are able to number them." And He said to him, "So shall your descendants be."
> And he believed in the Lord, and He accounted it to him for righteousness.

It seems that as quickly as God spoke to Abraham, Abraham was quick to believe Him. This allowed God to declare him righteous. Faith has great power with God. Whoever will believe Him quickly, without fighting and questioning, is held in high esteem before the Lord. As someone once said, "Being believed is God's greatest joy. Being doubted, however, is His greatest pain."

The Lord is looking for those who will believe Him. Those with childlike hearts will simply take Him at His Word and allow His Spirit and presence to move among them. They don't have to understand everything intellectually. They are those given to what bears witness in the Spirit. They know they can trust the Holy Spirit to guide them into all truth.

These are the ones who will believe others who report having seen the Lord. Of course, I am speaking of those who know the Lord and have had real encounters with Him; I am not speaking of the deceivers whom Jesus referred to in Matthew 24, when He spoke of false christs and prophets who would falsely claim to have seen Him. These we must reject and even expose as misguided and deceived. But here, I mean those who have had genuine encounters with the Lord. Mark 16:9–14 shows the reluctance of the disciples to believe those whom Jesus had appeared to after His death and resurrection:

> Now when He rose early on the first day of the week, He appeared first to Mary Magdalene, out of whom He had cast seven demons. She went and told those who had been with Him, as they mourned and wept. And when they heard that He was alive and had been seen by her, they did not believe.
>
> After that, He appeared in another form to two of them as they walked and went into the country. And they went and told it to the rest, but they did not believe them either.
>
> Later He appeared to the eleven as they sat at the table; and He rebuked their unbelief and hardness of heart, because they did not believe those who had seen Him after He had risen.

These disciples who had walked with Jesus were having a difficult time believing others whom the Lord had appeared to. This is so often true for us as well. Many times, we are just like Thomas, who says he will not believe unless Jesus appears to him personally. Jesus had appeared to the disciples while Thomas was not there, and in John 20:25–29 Thomas declares that unless he sees the Lord Himself, he will not believe:

> The other disciples therefore said to him, "We have seen the Lord."
>
> So he said to them, "Unless I see in His hands the print of the nails, and put my finger into the print of the nails, and put my hand into His side, I will not believe."
>
> And after eight days His disciples were again inside, and Thomas with them. Jesus came, the doors being shut, and stood in the midst, and said, "Peace to you!" Then He said to Thomas, "Reach your finger here, and look at My hands; and reach your hand here, and put it into My side. Do not be unbelieving, but believing."
>
> And Thomas answered and said to Him, "My Lord and my God!"
>
> Jesus said to him, "Thomas, because you have seen Me, you have believed. Blessed are those who have not seen and yet have believed."

The Lord in His kindness and mercy appears to Thomas and the disciples again, and He does for Thomas just as this doubting disciple demanded. He also lets Thomas and the others know that while it is awesome to see and believe, there is great blessing in having so much faith that seeing is unnecessary to believing.

This is where God would bring us—that we would believe at the witness of the Holy Spirit, rather than demanding to see. When we walk in this realm of faith, it is pleasing and accept-able to the Lord. It actually excites the Lord's heart over us. Can we believe because others have seen Him and bring their report? Can we believe because the Holy Spirit bears witness that this is true? Then we become believers who are quick to believe, and whom the Holy Spirit can move with freely.

## Unbelievers Drawn by Signs

Paul also mentions the *unbelievers*, or those who believe not. This is where Scripture seems to contradict itself. We saw in 1 Corinthians 14:22 that tongues are for a sign to those who believe not. Then we are told in verse 23 that if everyone is speaking in tongues in a church setting and an unbeliever comes in, he or she will think we are crazy. So which is it? Are tongues designed to convince unbelievers of the reality of Jesus, or do they confuse unbelievers who do not understand?

Of course, the answer is that tongues have the potential to do both. We see in the original introduction of tongues in the New Testament that the disciples were actually speaking the various known languages of different cultures without having learned them. Acts 2:6–12 gives us a detailed account of all the different nations, languages and dialects the disciples' gift of tongues represented:

> And when this sound occurred, the multitude came together, and were confused, because everyone heard them speak in his own language. Then they were all amazed and marveled, saying to one another, "Look, are not all these who speak Galileans? And how is it that we hear, each in our own language in which we were born? Parthians and Medes and Elamites, those dwelling in Mesopotamia, Judea and Cappadocia, Pontus and Asia, Phrygia and Pamphylia, Egypt and the parts of Libya adjoining Cyrene, visitors from Rome, both Jews and proselytes, Cretans and Arabs—we hear them speaking in our own tongues the wonderful works of God." So they were all amazed and perplexed, saying to one another, "Whatever could this mean?"

The initial baptism of the Holy Spirit and the release of tongues allowed the disciples to speak in clear languages that others understood. I count at least seventeen different groups mentioned here who heard the disciples from Galilee speaking understandably in languages previously unknown to them. It was reported that the tongues people were hearing were espousing the wonderful works of God and giving glory to Him. This caused all these different groups to be confused, amazed, marveled and perplexed. These hearers would have been categorized as unbelievers, and what they heard ultimately caused them to ask, "Whatever could this mean?" The Lord used this manifestation of tongues to create an interest in the lives of these who did not believe in who Jesus was.

Many times, an unbeliever's journey to becoming a believer begins with questions. This is why Peter said in 1 Peter 3:15, "But sanctify the Lord God in your hearts, and always be ready to give a defense to everyone who asks you a reason for the hope that is in you, with meekness and fear." At times, the Lord uses the supernatural to bring people to a place of questioning. We must be ready to answer the questions of these unbelievers, if we are to see them born again and converted.

This is what Peter did on the Day of Pentecost. He took the occasion of people asking a question, and he preached a sermon to answer it. The result was that three thousand people were born again in one day. A great harvest of souls resulted because of a question created through the supernatural manifestation of tongues.

It is my opinion that the 120 believers who began speaking other cultures' languages supernaturally probably did not know what they were saying. They simply

*Many times, an unbeliever's journey to becoming a believer begins with questions.*

113

spoke as the Holy Spirit gave them utterance. They allowed the rivers of living water to flow from their innermost being, out of their mouths, in the form of tongues. This allowed God to unveil a miracle that grasped the attention of people from multiple cultures. The question that began as "What does this mean?" became a new question in Acts 2:37: "Now when they heard this, they were cut to the heart, and said to Peter and the rest of the apostles, 'Men and brethren, what shall we do?'"

With the backdrop of witnessing the disciples' supernatural ability to speak languages they had not learned, conviction fell upon these unbelievers when Peter preached. All these who were saved and born again came into the Kingdom of God because the supernatural realm of tongues made them pay attention. Without this display, they would have had no interest. God used tongues to create a platform for Peter and the others to preach from. Evangelism becomes easy when the supernatural display of God is present. It creates questions in the hearts and minds of people, opening them to the reality of who Jesus is. This is one of the ways that tongues are used to convince unbelievers of their need for Jesus.

Another way is having tongues and the interpretation of tongues operate in the setting of a service. God will use tongues with interpretation to bring people to the Lord. Again, we are told that if an unbeliever comes into a church setting and everyone is speaking in tongues, he or she will leave and say everyone is crazy. This could give the Gospel of the Lord Jesus a bad name, so Paul's instruction was that the Church needed to be aware of this and *use* tongues beneficially to reach the lost. The issue was not that the believers *shouldn't* speak in tongues in a church service; it was that they needed to couple this gift with the gift of interpretation, which would allow tongues to have an impact on the lost.

We will look more closely in chapter 12 at how the interpretation of tongues works, but suffice it to say here that when tongues are in operation in a church service, there should be interpretation. Paul speaks of this in 1 Corinthians 14:5:

> I wish you all spoke with tongues, but even more that you prophesied; for he who prophesies is greater than he who speaks with tongues, unless indeed he interprets, that the church may receive edification.

In his efforts to make the Corinthian church more effective, Paul seeks to help them use the gifts of the Holy Spirit in a better way. He admonishes them that if someone speaks in tongues in a church setting, it should be interpreted. This will build up the Church and will encourage everyone in attendance.

Without tongues being interpreted, unbelievers will not be impacted. This is because they don't understand what is being spoken. Unlike what happened on the Day of Pentecost, in most church settings the tongues in operation are not understood by the masses because they are indeed unknown tongues. Perhaps they are languages from earth that no one in attendance knows. Maybe they are languages of angels, as we mentioned earlier. They could even be languages from the past that are no longer used in the earth. Whatever they are, they need interpretation so they can be useful among those who are present. Paul is therefore encouraging the interpretation of tongues to operate in this kind of occurrence. This interpretation is the supernatural ability to relate, using the language of the culture in attendance, whatever has been said. This way the Church is edified, and any unbelievers present will witness a supernatural gift in operation that might make them wonder, ask questions and discover who Jesus is.

I will mention one caveat to all of this. Many times, in coming before the Lord in a church setting, you might hear people praying, worshiping or singing in tongues on a personal level, right where they are. This kind of tongues does not require interpretation. Only when someone is given the right to speak out in tongues for all to hear in a service does an interpretation become necessary. In contrast, many believers simply use their gift of tongues to worship and intercede in private prayer in a corporate church setting. They are in actuality stirring themselves up in their most holy faith, as Jude 19–21 admonishes us to do:

> These [mockers] are sensual persons, who cause divisions, not having the Spirit. But you, beloved, building yourselves up on your most holy faith, praying in the Holy Spirit, keep yourselves in the love of God, looking for the mercy of our Lord Jesus Christ unto eternal life.

We are to move ourselves away from a sensual perspective that can cause divisions, to a spiritual place caused by praying in the Spirit. Divisions are created by people who are sensitive in a negative way. The word *sensual* here is the Greek word *psuchikos*, meaning "to be sensitive," with the idea of being easily offended. Perhaps we might say "wearing our feelings on our shoulders." The reason this is relatable here is because people like this can cause divisions. Scripture recognizes praying in the Holy Spirit or tongues as a way to combat our tendencies toward being overly sensitive. Instead of becoming separated, we become empowered in our faith instead.

This is why, whether in private worship or in a church setting, we can pray in the spirit and speak in tongues on an individual level and it does not require interpretation. If, however, there is a speaking out in tongues that grabs the attention of others who are present, it must be interpreted. Again, we will delve more into this later, but God will use this combined gifting of tongues and interpretation to impact the unbelievers.

## The Unlearned Made Hungry

The other group Paul mentions in addition to believers and un-believers is *the unlearned*. The unlearned would be those who are believers, but who do not have an awareness and knowledge of the gifts of the Holy Spirit, including tongues. This would include a large group of Christians today. It appears that this group existed in Paul's day as well. There were believers who had been saved, but they had not been baptized in the Holy Spirit. We see this in Acts 19:2, where Paul encounters disciples who know nothing of the Holy Spirit. As we saw, he also speaks of the unlearned in 1 Corinthians 14:23, in connection to un-believers who will not understand the operation of tongues without interpretation. Yet when tongues and interpretation function properly in a corporate setting, this unlearned group can be touched and empowered.

The word *unlearned* in the Greek is *idiotes*. Clearly, this is where we get our word *idiot* from. The simple meaning of *idiotes*, however, is "an ignorant or a private person." In other words, this is someone who does not know what those who have experi-enced the things of the Holy Spirit on a given level know. It does not mean that these unlearned people are hostile or are against something. It just means that they have not yet been afforded the privilege of encountering the Holy Spirit and His manifestations in the same dimension as those around them. The part of the definition meaning the unlearned are private people involves the idea that they simply have not been exposed to these giftings and phenomena. Paul is encouraging the Church to be aware of these unlearned people and allow the gifts of the Holy Spirit to flow in such a way that the unlearned are made hungry by them to experience the Lord and His presence in a deeper realm.

The wise leader of a ministry or church will be aware that at any time, the unlearned can be present, and they do not yet realize the things they could know about the Holy Spirit. We are always to be considerate of them, or else we might use the gifts of the Spirit in such a way that it scares them, making them uncomfortable and perhaps even causing them to leave before they are influenced and drawn by what they see. This is what Paul is warning of in 1 Corinthians 14:23, when he says such people could say we are out of our minds. Whenever something happens in a service that would not happen in a "traditional" church setting, I have always found it helpful to stop and explain what is going on. I have discovered that a simple explanation goes a long way in alleviating people's fears or discomfort. With a little explanation, we can allow the Holy Spirit's movement while not running people off before we see them impacted and touched.

It is the heart of Jesus to bring people into new realms of experience in Him. We are told that we are to go from faith to faith. As the righteous of the Lord, through faith we move from revelation to revelation of God and His ways: "For in it [the Gospel] the righteousness of God is revealed from faith to faith; as it is written, 'The just shall live by faith'" (Romans 1:17). God means for the unlearned to have deeper and deeper encounters with Him. We all are to be affected more and more with the glory of His presence. As this happens, we are transformed into the image of the One who created us. This requires instructing the unlearned ones. Our patient instruction of those who don't know the deep things of God can allow them to come into new places of encounter with the Lord.

*It is the heart of Jesus to bring people into new realms of experience in Him. We are told that we are to go from faith to faith.*

In 2 Timothy 2:24–25, we see the proper posture to have toward those who might be unlearned. If we could adopt this posture rather than insisting on our own rights as the Spirit-filled Church, we might see more of the unlearned being brought into a deeper place:

> And a servant of the Lord must not quarrel but be gentle to all, able to teach, patient, in humility correcting those who are in opposition, if God perhaps will grant them repentance, so that they may know the truth.

Notice the heart we are to have toward those who might even stand in opposition. We are to approach them as servants, not quarreling, but patiently teaching and instructing them. Wow, this just runs over with a passion and heart to love people into a deeper place in God! When we actually minister in such a way through the life, power and love of the Lord, people are drawn into new encounters with Him. The unlearned become those who are growing in the knowledge and grace of who our Lord is.

## No Longer Just Theology

As I am writing all of this, I can hear the protest of those who desire a Holy Ghost blowout. They are saying that we must not compromise the move of the Holy Spirit. I can hear them reasoning that if people in attendance at a service are hungry, they will get past anything that might offend them.

This mentality goes against what the apostle Paul was teaching us. I am all for the unbridled, unrestrained move of the Holy Spirit. Yet I believe that we must always be conscious of these three groups who could be in our midst at any time: believers, unbelievers and the unlearned. We are responsible to minister to and seek to apprehend all these groups.

May the Lord give us the wisdom to do this through different styles of services, through answering people's questions, through teaching the proper things with patience, and through simply being sensitive (in a good way) to where people are. If we can do this, we can see many folks brought into new places of the Holy Spirit and His manifestations. Lives will be changed, and no longer will the things of God be just theology to these people, who will instead become experiential and practiced. As a result, we will become an empowered Church that is administering its anointing with wisdom and delight!

*Seven*

# A PERSONAL PRAYER LANGUAGE

When we think of speaking in tongues, we must make the distinction between a public release of this gift and that which is private. There is a difference between speaking in tongues in a service or a public worship meeting and praying in tongues in my own individual life. Whereas the apostle Paul placed restrictions and boundaries on how he preferred to see this gift operate in public, there were none of these restrictions on our private prayer life. In fact, I believe that the gift of tongues first and foremost benefits us in developing and operating in our own prayer times with God.

One of the main reasons the Holy Spirit fills us is to empower us in prayer. Romans 8:19–23 shows that the Holy Spirit releases groanings through us to bring forth the ultimate event of history, the resurrection of the dead:

> For the earnest expectation of the creation eagerly waits for the revealing of the sons of God. For the creation was subjected to

futility, not willingly, but because of Him who subjected it in hope; because the creation itself also will be delivered from the bondage of corruption into the glorious liberty of the children of God. For we know that the whole creation groans and labors with birth pangs together until now. Not only that, but we also who have the firstfruits of the Spirit, even we ourselves groan within ourselves, eagerly waiting for the adoption, the redemption of our body.

Creation itself is groaning to be free of the bondage it was put under when Adam fell and transgressed in the Garden of Eden. God allowed His creation to be subdued under bondage, with the hope that one day it would be delivered back into glorious liberty. Notice that this will occur when the children of God are brought out of bondage and into that great place of liberty. It is God's people coming out of bondage that will liberate creation as well. We are told this will happen at the redemption of our bodies, the resurrection from the dead that takes place when Jesus comes back. The dead will rise when He comes back with a shout, the voice of the archangel and the trumpet of God. As 1 Thessalonians 4:15–18 clearly shows, this is no silent catching away; it is quite noisy and attention grabbing!

For this we say to you by the word of the Lord, that we who are alive and remain until the coming of the Lord will by no means precede those who are asleep. For the Lord Himself will descend from heaven with a shout, with the voice of an archangel, and with the trumpet of God. And the dead in Christ will rise first. Then we who are alive and remain shall be caught up together with them in the clouds to meet the Lord in the air. And thus we shall always be with the Lord. Therefore comfort one another with these words.

When this takes place, our bodies will be redeemed and the earth will be released from the curse and bondage it has labored under since the days of Adam. This is very certain. Notice, however, that until this happens, there is a *groaning* from the Holy Spirit through us that agrees with the groaning of creation. These groanings are birth pangs that will bring forth the purposes of God in the earth—even the ultimate purpose of His redemption of our bodies, the earth and all of creation. God's purposes are birthed through the groanings of the Holy Spirit in us. As we have already established, this process involves operating in tongues as our prayer language. Through tongues, we can groan with the groanings of God. The firstfruits of the Holy Spirit in our lives empower us to groan in prayer to see God's plans accomplished.

## Partnering with God

The Lord has graced us with such a high and noble call that He allows us to partner with Him. What an amazing thought! The groaning of God through the power of the Holy Spirit can bring forth amazing things. It took groans to bring the children of Israel out of Egypt. Exodus 2:23–25 shows that the groaning, sighs and cries of God's people caused Him to send Moses as the deliverer:

> Now it happened in the process of time that the king of Egypt died. Then the children of Israel groaned because of the bondage, and they cried out; and their cry came up to God because of the bondage. So God heard their groaning, and God remembered His covenant with Abraham, with Isaac, and with Jacob. And God looked upon the children of Israel, and God acknowledged them.

When God heard the people's groans, it caused Him to remember His covenant, look on Israel and acknowledge them. The groaning from the depths of His people set this in motion.

Through the prayer language of tongues, God empowers us to groan. This is part of unlocking the events that will shape and determine history. We are incapable of praying on this level in and of ourselves. Through the power of the Holy Spirit and tongues, however, we can groan with the unction of the Holy Spirit to give birth to God's will.

*Through the prayer language of tongues, God empowers us to groan. This is part of unlocking the events that will shape and determine history.*

In Scripture, this is seen as *travail*. Romans 8:22 calls it *birth pangs*. This is a good picture of what transpires as the Holy Spirit moves through us in prayer. Before a woman can travail in birth and bring forth a child, she must first conceive. This is likewise true when we are carrying the burden of the Lord in prayer. There is always a conception in us first. Out of intimacy with God, we are impregnated with His burdens, desires and concerns. This is a precious thing. He entrusts these things only to those who carry His heart. Just as a woman must care for the seed/child she is pregnant with, so must we. When we are carrying a seed from the Lord, we must cherish and nurture it. Paul told Timothy in 2 Timothy 1:14 to guard, keep and protect what was placed in him: "That good thing which was committed to you, keep by the Holy Spirit who dwells in us." This is true for the things in us that we are entrusted to birth through prayer.

There then comes the time when a woman goes into labor and begins to travail. What has previously been some slight discomfort now becomes intense and rigorous. I have watched my wife, Mary, give birth to six children. I remember when our first was born. I was only 21 years old and had no idea what I was about to witness. I remember going to the hospital, where the first thing we encountered in the birthing area was a woman screaming. I had never heard such cries. As a young husband who had never given any thought to the birthing process, I was traumatized. I remember it to this day.

As Mary began her labor process, I watched this young woman I had married go into great travail. She did not scream like the other woman (I was thankful for that), but she did go through the process of labor for several hours. As her labor progressed, her body dilated in preparation for birthing our son. The travail Mary was in caused everything to become rightly positioned inside her for the birth. The baby in her womb shifted and moved into the necessary place so that he could be born into the world.

It then came time for Mary to push. The travail had served to prepare her body and the baby so she could push our son out, giving birth to him. The Bible uses this analogy to picture our prayer under the unction and presence of the Holy Spirit. Our prayer languages are a big part of this birthing process. We pray in tongues to steward what is in us. We pray in tongues to prepare what we are carrying. We pray in tongues as we travail. Then we pray in tongues to push something forth and give birth to it in the spirit realm. What happens with the birthing process in the natural is an accurate description of this process in the spiritual.

## Called to Travail

Travailing in the Spirit is the sign that the time has come to birth the promises of God fully into reality. Without this process, we cannot see the birthing of God's will, purposes and promises into reality through us. In John 16:20–22, we see Jesus instructing His disciples about the travail they will go through and what it will produce:

> Most assuredly, I say to you that you will weep and lament, but the world will rejoice; and you will be sorrowful, but your sorrow will be turned into joy. A woman, when she is in labor, has sorrow because her hour has come; but as soon as she has given birth to the child, she no longer remembers the anguish, for joy that a human being has been born into the world. Therefore you now have sorrow; but I will see you again and your heart will rejoice, and your joy no one will take from you.

Jesus was speaking of what His disciples would go through while He was being crucified, and He likened what they would experience during His death, burial and resurrection to travail. Notice that the end result of their travail would be the birthing of something that could not be taken away from them. Jesus said the sorrow they experienced would be forgotten and would turn to joy once this birth occurred.

I remember that the same was true after Mary had given birth to our firstborn son. They rolled her out of the delivery room she had labored in (this was before the days of birthing rooms), and I stood next to her gurney while they prepared a hospital room for her. I had just watched the whole ordeal, witnessing her great pain and everything that went with the birthing process. After all that, I was certain Mary had just given birth to our one and only child. Who would want to go through that again?

As we waited in the hospital hallway, I said something to Mary like, "Well, at least that's over."

To my amazement, she looked at me and said, "I would do it again!"

*What?* I thought. *Are you out of your mind? Don't you remember the pain, despair, hurt and sorrow you were going through less than an hour ago? You would do it again?*

Later, when I read John 16:20–22, I realized the birthing process Mary experienced took place exactly the way Jesus had described it. All her pain and sorrow were forgotten because a child had just been born into the earth. Likewise, the disciples' pain and sorrow were part of the process as Jesus laid down His life for us. Yet He would rise and come out of the grave, and the disciples would experience such joy that it would cause their sorrow to be remembered no more. This is what our travail in the Holy Spirit can do. We can birth something that will produce great joy in us, but also in the world.

On the other hand, Isaiah 23:4 shows us that a lack of travail is a judgment from God: "Be ashamed, O Sidon; for the sea has spoken, the strength of the sea, saying, 'I do not labor, nor bring forth children; neither do I rear young men, nor bring up virgins.'" A lack of travail and labor to bring forth life is a sign of the Lord's displeasure.

Contrary to that, when the Lord gives us the honor of carrying something from Him in our spirits and travailing to bring it forth, it is a sign of His pleasure. Isaiah 53:11 even makes note of this concerning Jesus and what He would do for us: "He [the Father] shall see the labor of His soul [Jesus], and be satisfied. By His knowledge My righteous Servant shall justify many, for He shall bear their iniquities." God the Father was satisfied when He witnessed the labor and travail of Jesus' soul, which took place on the cross, but also ahead of the cross. Jesus' travail beforehand was intense as He wrestled with His own flesh, the powers of darkness and even His disciples' lack of commitment. Luke 22:39–45 shows how all of this threw His soul into travail and labor:

Coming out, He went to the Mount of Olives, as He was accustomed, and His disciples also followed Him. When He came to the place, He said to them, "Pray that you may not enter into temptation."

And He was withdrawn from them about a stone's throw, and He knelt down and prayed, saying, "Father, if it is Your will, take this cup away from Me; nevertheless not My will, but Yours, be done." Then an angel appeared to Him from heaven, strengthening Him. And being in agony, He prayed more earnestly. Then His sweat became like great drops of blood falling down to the ground.

When He rose up from prayer, and had come to His disciples, He found them sleeping from sorrow.

As Jesus wrestled through prayer, His disciples slept. Notice that so great was the travail of His soul that He sweat drops of blood. Medical experts tell us this is a sign of unbelievable anguish experienced by only a few. Jesus' soul was pressing through concerning what He was about to do for us. This was the travail and labor God witnessed, and it brought Him satisfaction. We speak of Jesus' suffering on the cross, yet this travail beforehand was also some of the suffering in the atoning work of God. When Scripture says that God was satisfied, it means that every legal condition necessary for our redemption was being met. This included Jesus' travail of soul on our behalf.

My point is that we are called to travail. This involves the use of tongues. We can use the prayer language God has granted us to express the longing of our heart to heaven, but also to express the longing of His heart through us. Unimaginable things can be accomplished out of our travail in our prayer language. The destiny of nations can even be shifted and arranged as we labor and travail. I believe Isaiah 66:7–8 implies that the purposes of the Lord cannot occur without the travail of God's people before Him:

> Before she was in labor, she gave birth; before her pain came, she delivered a male child. Who has heard such a thing? Who has seen such things? Shall the earth be made to give birth in one day? Or shall a nation be born at once? For as soon as Zion was in labor, she gave birth to her children.

God is making a promise here that He will bring forth His will, even in regard to the nations. I think this passage seems to say, however, that this cannot happen without travail and labor. Only when labor and travail come will what God wants in the nations occur. This means that God must have a travailing people who know how to use tongues to stand in the gap and pray. Their travail will birth events that are necessary to God's will and promises being fulfilled.

## The Added Benefits of Tongues

Praying in tongues on a personal level is also associated with other significant benefits. I will cover these added benefits as individual topics in the chapters ahead, but for the time being let me at least mention them briefly. The first thing the gift of tongues does is bring encouragement into our spirit and life. First Corinthians 14:4 tells us, "He who speaks in a tongue edifies himself, but he who prophesies edifies the church." When we speak in tongues, we are releasing encouragement and assurance into the deepest part of our being.

Romans 8:16 clarifies this even further: "The Spirit Himself bears witness with our spirit that we are children of God." When Scripture speaks of the Spirit *bearing witness*, this is legal language. In other words, the Spirit is releasing a testimony to us that we belong to Jesus. When we pray in tongues, we become assured in our spirit that we are the Lord's. This is the Holy Spirit's affirming and confirming ministry to us. According to Ephesians 1:13–14, we are sealed with the Holy Spirit of promise until the day of our absolute redemption:

> In Him you also trusted, after you heard the word of truth, the gospel of your salvation; in whom also, having believed, you were sealed with the Holy Spirit of promise, who is the guarantee of our inheritance until the redemption of the purchased possession, to the praise of His glory.

The Holy Spirit is the guarantee of our inheritance. He seals us until the redemption of God's purchased possession, which we are. We have been bought by the blood of the Lamb, so we belong to Jesus. Sealing us, the Holy Spirit confirms to us that this is, in fact, true. An awareness of this comes to us when we pray in tongues. That which is unspeakable testifies to us, which encourages and builds us up.

A second thing that happens when we exercise our prayer language is that revelation comes. When we pray in tongues, 1 Corinthians 14:2 tells us that we are speaking mysteries: "For he who speaks in a tongue does not speak to men but to God, for no one understands him; however, in the spirit he speaks mysteries." Even though we may not know what we are saying in our prayer language, we are actually speaking mysteries in the Spirit.

Many times, the mysteries we speak can be hidden truths. We will talk more later about that, but suffice it to say here that these mysteries are things that have been kept hidden until the appointed time for them to be revealed. As we pray in tongues, we speak mysteries that our understanding can begin to unlock. This allows us to begin to perceive things that have been hidden from us until the appointed time. Things are revealed as we pray in tongues. Our prayer language before the Lord starts to unlock our spiritual senses, which allows us to discern the deep things of God that were previously hidden.

A third added benefit of praying in the gift of tongues is that it allows us to worship on an accelerated level. As 1 Corinthians 14:16–17 tells us, when we pray in tongues, we give thanks well to God: "Otherwise, if you bless with the spirit . . . you indeed give thanks well." This word *well* is the Greek word *kalos*, which means "with beauty" or "beautiful." Our prayer in tongues is beautiful praise and thanks to the Lord.

> *Our prayer language before the Lord starts to unlock our spiritual senses, which allows us to discern the deep things of God that were previously hidden.*

Psalm 66:2 speaks of making God's praise glorious: "Sing out the honor of His name; make His praise glorious." When we pray in tongues, we can be releasing praise to the Lord that is beautiful and glorious. It is perfect praise that speaks to and satisfies the heart of God. When our praise is of the perfected kind, it allows the Lord's pleasure to flow over us.

A fourth thing that can happen when we pray in tongues is that we release a blessing. We just saw that 1 Corinthians 14:16 says "you bless with the spirit." Even though blessing and giving thanks are connected, blessing carries a little different idea. When I bless something, I am releasing a spiritual force that causes something good to come on someone. The word *bless* here is the Greek word *eulogeo*, which means "to speak well of, to invoke a benediction upon, to prosper." So when we bless, we are setting a blessing on someone or something that will allow that person or endeavor to prosper. This is the power of praying in tongues. We are causing someone to move forward with the blessing of God on his or her life. What a powerful idea connected to praying in tongues!

The fifth and final idea or benefit is that when we operate in the gift of tongues, we speak to God and not to man. We are told very clearly in 1 Corinthians 14:2 that the gift of tongues is a vertical declaration, not a horizontal one: "For he who speaks in a tongue does not speak to men but to God, for no one understands him; however, in the spirit he speaks mysteries." When someone prays in tongues, then, it is a prayer of worship, thanks or blessing toward God. It is not God speaking to us; it is us speaking to God. We will look at this more in depth in chapter 12, but this is true in our prayer language and also in any release of tongues in a church setting.

As we operate in our personal prayer language of tongues, we can begin to expect and operate in a greater release of adoration, requests, prayer and worship to the One who is worthy of it all. The gift of tongues becomes a means to declare all of this in a greater form than we ever have before.

# *Eight*

# PARTNERING WITH OUR INTERCESSOR

As a result of His position as our Great High Priest, Jesus is our Intercessor. He occupies this wonderful place for us. We tend to exalt in and marvel at what Jesus did for us by His atoning work on the cross. We major on His death, burial and resurrection. As wonderful as this is, however, we also need a new awareness of His present-day ministry to us. Even though Jesus died to provide all things for us, He is now praying and interceding for us, so that we would enter into everything He provided. He is the Mediator of the New Covenant. He is the High Priest of the confession of our faith. He is the Intercessor standing on our behalf before God. He is our Advocate with the Father.

All these terms for Him are similar in declaring who Jesus presently is for us. Yet I want to zero in on the term *Intercessor* as we learn to agree with what He is praying for us. Jesus' present-day ministry is not a separate act disconnected from who we are. We who are yet on the earth agree with His intercession through the power and ministry of the Holy Spirit in us. The gift of tongues is a big part of the agreement we are actively involved in.

Romans 8:34 tells us Jesus is presently interceding for us: "Who is he who condemns? It is Christ who died, and furthermore is also risen, who is even at the right hand of God, who also makes intercession for us." Jesus is not condemning us for our sins and shortcomings; instead, He is interceding for us. We must understand what it means to intercede. When people intercede, that means they are representing another person before the Lord. As a result of their position being recognized, their words are deemed as the words of another.

*Jesus pleads our case before God, and God hears Him. This is what He is doing as our Intercessor.*

This is the whole idea of an attorney representing a client, and it is why 1 John 2:1 calls Jesus our Advocate: "My little children, these things I write to you, so that you may not sin. And if anyone sins, we have an Advocate with the Father, Jesus Christ the righteous." Through His advocacy, Jesus is representing us before the Father. Because the Son has such favor before Him, the Father will accept Jesus' cry on our behalf. Jesus pleads our case before God, and God hears Him. This is what He is doing as our Intercessor.

## Four Things Working for Us

Romans 8:34, which we just read, says there are four things working with Jesus on our behalf: He died, He is risen, He is at the right hand of God and He is making intercession. These four things allow Jesus to impact the spirit world for us as He stands before the Father in our stead. The first thing, His death for us, was the ultimate act of obedience. He died because He loves us, but His greatest motivation in making that sacrifice was His complete obedience to God His Father. Philippians 2:8–9 tells us the esteem that God has for Jesus because of this tremendous act of obedience:

> And being found in appearance as a man, He humbled Himself and became obedient to the point of death, even the death of the cross. Therefore God also has highly exalted Him and given Him the name which is above every name.

Notice that God has highly exalted Jesus because of His great feat of dying in obedience. Jesus' death not only purchased salvation for us; it granted Him a great position with God, from which He can intercede on our behalf.

The second thing working for us is that Jesus is risen. This means He is alive forevermore. His resurrection means He won, so He is interceding for us from a place of great victory. Death and the devil could not defeat Him. He rose from the dead, never to die again, and He is the victorious King who reigns forevermore.

The third thing that works in our favor is that Jesus is at the right hand of God. This position the Father granted Him is one of ultimate authority and power. Because Jesus became a man, He now sits at the right hand of God to represent us before Him. He knows the Father's demands, but also the needs of humankind. This gives Him the unique ability to act as the Mediator between God and us, according to 1 Timothy 2:5–6: "For there is one God and one Mediator between God and men, the Man Christ Jesus, who gave Himself a ransom for all, to be testified in due time." Sitting at the right hand of God, Jesus represents both the Godhead and humankind. He has the ability to secure for us the benefits of the salvation He purchased, while representing the values, virtues and demands of who God is. This is the position He holds.

The fourth thing working for us is that Jesus is making intercession for us. Notice that His intercession is *for us*. He loves us dearly. All that He is presently doing is done on our behalf and for us. This is the exalted place He holds as our recognized Intercessor who represents us before God. This kind of representation before God is a tremendous principle of prayer. We can even represent one another this way, according to 1 John 5:16:

> If anyone sees his brother sinning a sin which does not lead to death, he will ask, and He will give him life for those who commit sin not leading to death. There is sin leading to death. I do not say that he should pray about that.

We can intercede before God for each other, as Jesus does for us. Before we talk about that a little more, let me note that I believe the sin leading to death mentioned here speaks of something spiritual. It does not speak of physical death, but rather of spiritual death, which is eternal separation from God. Let's look for a moment at this kind of sin before we move on.

## The Unpardonable Sin

The Bible seems clear that there is an unpardonable sin called *blasphemy against the Holy Spirit*. I mentioned this briefly in chapter 2, but let's look again at Matthew 12:31–32, which talks about this unforgivable sin:

> Therefore I say to you, every sin and blasphemy will be forgiven men, but the blasphemy against the Spirit will not be forgiven men. Anyone who speaks a word against the Son of

Man, it will be forgiven him; but whoever speaks against the Holy Spirit, it will not be forgiven him, either in this age or in the age to come.

If we were guilty of speaking against the Holy Spirit and calling His operation the works of the devil, it could have grave consequences. Hebrews 6:4–8 also tells us that if someone has had massive encounters with the Lord and yet chooses to walk away from Him, this, too, can have dire results:

> For it is impossible for those who were once enlightened, and have tasted the heavenly gift, and have become partakers of the Holy Spirit, and have tasted the good word of God and the powers of the age to come, if they fall away, to renew them again to repentance, since they crucify again for themselves the Son of God, and put Him to an open shame.
>
> For the earth which drinks in the rain that often comes upon it, and bears herbs useful for those by whom it is cultivated, receives blessing from God; but if it bears thorns and briers, it is rejected and near to being cursed, whose end is to be burned.

People can walk away from God and then find that they have no place to return to. Before you become terrified that you have done such a thing, let me assure you that if you care about it, you have not done it! Those who have done it are given over to a reprobate mind and simply don't care anymore. Romans 1:22–28 shows God giving such people over to a reprobate mind. They then give themselves over to all sorts of ungodly things with no sense of shame, guilt or even fear of what is to come, and the Holy Spirit has ceased to bring them conviction:

> Professing to be wise, they became fools, and changed the glory of the incorruptible God into an image made like corruptible man—and birds and four-footed animals and creeping things.

Therefore God also gave them up to uncleanness, in the lusts of their hearts, to dishonor their bodies among themselves, who exchanged the truth of God for the lie, and worshiped and served the creature rather than the Creator, who is blessed forever. Amen.

For this reason God gave them up to vile passions. For even their women exchanged the natural use for what is against nature. Likewise also the men, leaving the natural use of the woman, burned in their lust for one another, men with men committing what is shameful, and receiving in themselves the penalty of their error which was due.

And even as they did not like to retain God in their knowledge, God gave them over to a debased mind, to do those things which are not fitting.

In these few verses, we see God giving these people up and over three distinct times. Ultimately, they are given over to a *debased* mind. This is the Greek word *adokimos*, meaning "unapproved, rejected, castaway." As a result of this, they are incapable of sensing or feeling the conviction of the Holy Spirit. The Holy Spirit has ceased to wrestle with them and bring them to repentance.

This is a dreadful place for someone to reach, yet it seems a real possibility or else Scripture would not speak of it. Again, lest you be fearful that you have come to such a place, you must realize that if you still care, you have *not* committed this sin. Plus, the Bible lists five things you would have had to experience before you were even eligible to commit such a sin unto death. First, you would have been enlightened so that by revelation, you would have known who Jesus is. You would have been saved, just as by revelation Peter told Jesus that He was the Christ in Matthew 16:15–17:

He said to them, "But who do you say that I am?"

Simon Peter answered and said, "You are the Christ, the Son of the living God."

> Jesus answered and said to him, "Blessed are you, Simon Bar-Jonah, for flesh and blood has not revealed this to you, but My Father who is in heaven."

Jesus was excited because He realized that Peter had become able to receive revelation of who He was from the Father in heaven. Peter had become enlightened.

Second, for someone to fall away and sin unto death, that person must also have tasted of the heavenly gift. This means the things of heaven have had an impact on the person. He or she has encountered something that is not just earthly, but heavenly in nature, through which God has revealed His goodness and character.

Third, such people also must have partaken of the Holy Spirit, having received His filling and power. Fourth, they must have tasted the good word of God, experiencing His power and anointing as His word was ministered. Fifth and finally, they must have been touched by the powers of the world to come. This would mean they have seen and known the miraculous demonstration of God.

*If you are terrorized by the idea that you may have lost your salvation, the very fact that you have such a fear is proof that you have not done this!*

If someone has had this kind of witness about who Jesus is and yet chooses to turn away, he or she can be guilty of the unpardonable sin and be unable to return to God. This list would not apply to most believers today. Let me say it one more time: If you are terrorized by the idea that you may have *lost your salvation*, the very fact that you have such a fear is proof that you have not done this!

## Legal Representation before God

We already saw in 1 John 15:16 that, with the exception of this unpardonable sin, if someone sees someone else sinning, he or she can represent the sinner before the Father and see life be given to that person. What a marvelous thing! We have the power to step in and stand before the Lord on behalf of other people and secure life for them, when they might otherwise have experienced death. This is the power of intercession. If we can do this for each other as human beings, how much more can Jesus do this for us as our Intercessor?

To understand Jesus' intercession for us, we should know that it is legal in nature. Revelation 19:10 gives us some insight into who Jesus is and what He presently does as our Intercessor:

> And I fell at his feet to worship him. But he said to me, "See that you do not do that! I am your fellow servant, and of your brethren who have the testimony of Jesus. Worship God! For the testimony of Jesus is the spirit of prophecy."

As John encounters a heavenly being, he mistakenly falls down to worship him. He is told not to do this, because only God is worthy of worship. Then this heavenly being gives John the revelation that "the testimony of Jesus is the spirit of prophecy." I am aware that this revelation perhaps can mean several different things. One thing that stands out to me is that the heavenly being does not say "the testimony *about* Jesus," but rather "the testimony *of* Jesus." This would mean it was not someone or something speaking about Jesus, but rather was what Jesus Himself was saying.

Since what Jesus Himself is presently saying is called a *testimony*, it must therefore be taking place in a legal arena in heaven, or the spirit world. Everything has legal ramifications in the spirit world. Things happen based on the voices speaking before the Lord. For instance, Isaiah 54:17 shows the Lord saying this:

> No weapon formed against you shall prosper, and every tongue which rises against you in judgment you shall condemn. This is the heritage of the servants of the LORD, and their righteousness is from Me.

The word judgment here is the Hebrew word *mishpat*, meaning "a verdict pronounced judicially, a sentence." Please notice that a tongue or voice speaking is what would set a verdict against us in place. This is what allows a weapon like a curse, sickness, tragedy or anything negative to come against us. The weapon is the result of a tongue causing a judgment to be against us.

To deal with such a weapon, we must silence the tongue wielding it! We are told that silencing and condemning such a tongue is our honor. We have been granted a place before the Lord because of our birthright and heritage, and His righteousness in us. Everything in the spirit world is a result of the voices that are driving things. Jesus' *testimony* is His intercession, in His voice. That testimony on our behalf is granting the necessary evidence for good things to come our way. His voice is for us, granting the Father the legal right to move on our behalf as the Judge of all.

*Everything in the spirit world is a result of the voices that are driving things. Jesus' testimony is His intercession, in His voice.*

Hebrews 12:22–23 says we have come into a spiritual dimension where the Lord is sitting as Judge of all the earth:

> But you have come to Mount Zion and to the city of the living God, the heavenly Jerusalem, to an innumerable company of

angels, to the general assembly and church of the firstborn who are registered in heaven, to God the Judge of all, to the spirits of just men made perfect.

Since we have come to this place, we have the right to petition God within that expression of who He is as Judge, and in agreement with Jesus' testimony concerning us. We can pray and approach God as the Judge of all, because things work legally in the spirit world.

The result of all this is that the testimony of Jesus is His intercession. In other words, He is making a case concerning us, and our case is being heard before the Judge of all. Answered prayer is therefore God our Judge rendering a decision based on the testimony of Jesus on our behalf. With that understanding, we are told that the testimony of Jesus is the spirit of prophecy. This means that whatever Jesus is testifying concerning us becomes a prophetic unction we can began to pray and function from. The Holy Spirit takes the intercession/testimony of Jesus and deposits it in our spirit. We then began to move with a prophetic unction to pray and intercede. Our intercession is then in agreement with the intercession and testimony of Jesus.

This is why Romans 8:26–27 unveils the working of the Holy Spirit in regard to prayer:

> Likewise the Spirit also helps in our weaknesses. For we do not know what we should pray for as we ought, but the Spirit Himself makes intercession for us with groanings which cannot be uttered. Now He who searches the hearts knows what the mind of the Spirit is, because He makes intercession for the saints according to the will of God.

Notice that the Holy Spirit makes intercession in agreement with the will of God. He creates within us an unction/spirit of prophecy that empowers us to agree with the prayers of Jesus.

In this way, Jesus' intercession/testimony is shared among those joined to Him. Remember that He is the Head and we are the Body, according to Colossians 1:18: "And He is the head of the body, the church, who is the beginning, the firstborn from the dead, that in all things He may have the preeminence." The Body moves in agreement with the dictates of the Head. This is why we are told in 1 John 4:17 that we represent Jesus and even partake of His present-day ministry of intercession: "Love has been perfected among us in this: that we may have boldness in the day of judgment; because as He is, so are we in this world." This means that whatever He is presently doing, we are doing it, too. We get the privilege and honor of partaking of His present-day ministry of intercession through the prophetic unction of the Holy Spirit. The Holy Spirit takes the testimony of Jesus and allows us to travail together with Him.

Acts 1:8 gives us further insight into this phenomenon: "But you shall receive power when the Holy Spirit has come upon you; and you shall be witnesses to Me in Jerusalem, and in all Judea and Samaria, and to the end of the earth." We are promised power when the Holy Spirit comes on us—power for the purpose of being His witnesses. This word *witness* in the Greek is *martus*, and it means to be "a judicial witness." I am aware that the disciples gave witness through their preaching and the demonstration of power that flowed from them. Their witness was presenting evidence that Jesus is alive and not dead.

## The Dynamic Testimony of Tongues

In addition, I would also like to suggest that the disciples' witness was not just on earth, but was also in heaven. Notice that Jesus commissioned them to release their witness in Jerusalem, Judea, Samaria and the uttermost parts of the earth. These regions were held under demonic control. Before the disciples could manifest the Kingdom of God in these spheres in the earth, they first had to possess them in the realms of the spirit. This meant they had to see revoked in the courts of heaven the legal right of the demonic principalities that held these regions in bondage.

This is what Paul referred to in Ephesians 6:12: "For we do not wrestle against flesh and blood, but against principalities, against powers, against the rulers of the darkness of this age, against spiritual hosts of wickedness in the heavenly places." The way we wrestle against these forces and win the battle in the spiritual and heavenly realm is through legal testimony. Principalities and powers control and dominate various regions because they claim a legal right to do so. If this legal right is to be revoked, we must bring testimony before the judicial system of heaven. This is just as much being a witness of who Jesus is as performing a sign and wonder.

This, I believe, was part of the commissioning of the apostles. They were to give witness in heaven that would agree with the testimony of Jesus, which would cause the legal claims of the power of darkness to be revoked. The result would be that territories, cities and regions of the earth would start to be dominated by the Kingdom of God, not by the demonic. This is a big part of what we do when we operate as His witnesses. Our testimony/intercession, agreeing with Jesus' testimony, allows verdicts and decisions to be rendered in heaven. The result is that spheres of the earth are claimed again for the Kingdom of God.

A big part of our witness is speaking in tongues. Jesus said His disciples would be His witnesses to the end of the earth. When the Holy Spirit showed up on the Day of Pentecost, the dominant thing that took place was the filling with the Spirit and the manifestation of tongues. This would mean that the gift of tongues in operation was the giving of testimony both in earth and also in heaven.

One of the chief ways we give witness and agree with Jesus' testimony is through praying in the Holy Spirit, or in tongues. Even though we may not know what we are saying, we are releasing dynamic testimony before the judicial system of heaven. This allows God as Judge to render decisions for His will to be done in the earth.

Through tongues, we are petitioning this court setting of heaven in agreement with the testimony of Jesus. We are being His witnesses in and from the earth. We may not know everything that is happening in the unseen world, but we are moving by faith, through the unction of the Holy Spirit. The spirit of prophecy is taking the testimony of Jesus and allowing us to witness to who He is and what His passion is. What a glorious honor this is, as we pray in and through our prayer language of tongues to move things in heaven, that earth might be touched.

*Nine*

# DEFEATING
# THE THREE "Ds"

As I have taught in other places, the gift of tongues can be used mightily to destroy what I call the three "Ds," which are discouragement, depression and disillusionment. These are huge issues in the Body of Christ. Pastoring for 22 years and traveling extensively for many more, I have seen these three Ds wreaking havoc in people's lives and families. High-profile ministers have even committed suicide because they became too discouraged, depressed and disillusioned, and they saw no way out. What a sad and troubling thing to see their lives shortened, their families left in disarray and their church bodies strapped with seemingly unanswerable questions.

Yet as with all other things, the Bible does present solutions. I am in no way making light of or diminishing other people's struggles. In years gone by, I have faced my own set of battles. I do understand being in the throes of mental conflict, fear, depression and a sense of only doom in the present and for the future. But I have discovered a way out, and I cannot

147

underestimate the power of tongues as part of God's prescription and solution.

Let me first differentiate between these three Ds a little. *Discouragement* can be a momentary lapse of faith because of negative things that are touching our lives. If this is not overcome, then the next D can set in, *depression*, which is the result of believing a lie. Something begins to present itself as real, when in many cases it is not. When we don't effectively deal with these first two stages, then the third D, *disillusionment*, occurs. Loss of vision happens at this third stage. We then become hopeless and choose to give up.

None of these three Ds is the will of God. Believe it or not, the gift of tongues is at least part of God's answer for overcoming them. Two main Scriptures that clarify this are 1 Corinthians 14:4 and Jude 20–21, both of which we have talked about already. But here, they deserve another mention. The first Scripture tells us that we can edify ourselves: "He who speaks in a tongue edifies himself, but he who prophesies edifies the church." The second Scripture tells us that we are to build ourselves up: "But you, beloved, building yourselves up on your most holy faith, praying in the Holy Spirit, keep yourselves in the love of God, looking for the mercy of our Lord Jesus Christ unto eternal life."

*These three powerful things—faith, love and mercy—subdue the demonic powers of discouragement, depression and disillusionment.*

Notice that as we pray in the Holy Spirit, which is a reference to tongues, we build ourselves up in our most holy faith. Notice also that we keep ourselves in the love of God and His mercy. Faith, love and mercy are released to us as we pray in the Holy Spirit, which is why we are edified and built up. These three powerful things—faith, love and mercy—subdue the demonic powers of discouragement, depression and disillusionment.

## Faith Is Essential

Let's look at the faith, love and mercy that are set in motion over our lives as we pray in tongues. Faith is essential to overcoming the three Ds. Romans 10:17 tells us, "So then faith comes by hearing, and hearing by the word of God." The term for *word* here is the Greek word *rhema*, meaning "an utterance." The *rhema* word of God is not just the written word of the Bible; it is also the spoken word of God through the ministry of the Holy Spirit. This is what produces faith.

Abraham's faith was connected to a word he had heard from God, which is what kept him believing in faith for decades. Romans 4:17–18 shows us that Abraham was able to persevere and endure in his faith because of what he personally had heard God say:

> (As it is written, "I have made you a father of many nations") in the presence of Him whom he believed—God, who gives life to the dead and calls those things which do not exist as though they did; who, contrary to hope, in hope believed, so that he became the father of many nations, according to what was spoken, "So shall your descendants be."

Abraham had heard the Lord say, "So shall your descendants be." This ignited a faith in him that lasted for decades, until the promise came true.

When we pray in tongues, we unlock the potential to hear God speak His word to us. Out of our prayer language, our ability to hear is opened and the Lord's voice can begin to resonate in us. When we pray this way, we step into a place of the Spirit where hearing God is much easier and more accessible. The Holy Spirit is able to take even the written Word and speak it to us. Isaiah 55:10–11 reveals this, where it pictures the Word of God as rain and snow:

> For as the rain comes down, and the snow from heaven, and do not return there, but water the earth, and make it bring forth and bud, that it may give seed to the sower and bread to the eater, so shall My word be that goes forth from My mouth; it shall not return to Me void, but it shall accomplish what I please, and it shall prosper in the thing for which I sent it.

Rain would be the *rhema* word. It simply falls from heaven and waters the earth on impact. Yet snow in particular is a picture of the written Word, which is *logos* in the Greek. Rain simply waters the earth and causes things to grow. For the earth to benefit from snow's moisture, however, the snow must melt. This is a picture of God's *rhema* word coming from His *logos*. In other words, the Holy Spirit causes what is in the written Word to come alive as God's spoken and uttered word to us. This is like snow melting so that the moisture it contains waters the earth. This happens as we pray in tongues. Through praying in the spirit, the *logos* turns into the *rhema*. The written Word becomes the utterance of God to us. The snow melts, and the earth is watered. Our operation in tongues allows this to occur.

For me, this process occurs as I meditate on the *logos* of God while I pray in tongues. Suddenly, revelations come and enlighten my understanding. The result is that faith can erupt in my heart. Remember, faith is a result of hearing the *rhema* word of God. Tongues can be a major part of melting the snow so that *rhema* appears. This kind of faith will combat discouragement, depression and disillusionment.

We are to *live* by every word that proceeds from the mouth of God, according to Matthew 4:4: "It is written, 'Man shall not live by bread alone, but by every word that proceeds from the mouth of God.'" When we are told to *live* this way, Jesus is speaking of living the abundant life He has promised us. Living this kind of life beats the three Ds every time. We are not just to enjoy the natural provisions of God; real life comes from the faith that ignites in us when we are able to receive the proceeding word from God's mouth—the *rhema*. The gift of tongues facilitates its release.

## Love Is Absolute

We are also told that through praying in the Holy Spirit, we *keep ourselves in the love of God.* God's love is absolute. It is remarkably unchanging toward us, no matter what. Romans 8:36–39 makes some astounding statements about His love for us:

> As it is written:
> "For Your sake we are killed all day long;
> We are accounted as sheep for the slaughter."
> Yet in all these things we are more than conquerors through Him who loved us. For I am persuaded that neither death nor life, nor angels nor principalities nor powers, nor things present nor things to come, nor height nor depth, nor any other created thing, shall be able to separate us from the love of God which is in Christ Jesus our Lord.

Even when we go through persecution, hardship and trials, God's love is present. This passage declares that it is the awareness of His love that make us overcomers and conquerors in the midst of any afflictions. We are then told that absolutely nothing can separate us from the love God has for us through His Son, Christ Jesus.

You and I must believe that no matter what we *feel* like or even what we are struggling with emotionally, God's love has not changed. His love is steadfast and unchanging. With this said, remember that Jude 21 tells us to "keep yourselves in the love of God." In other words, God's love is present, but we must stay joined to it. We must *keep* our hearts and minds alert to the reality of God's ever-present care for us. We do this through praying in tongues.

As I pray in tongues, my understanding may be unfruitful, but my spirit is connecting to the Lord's lovingkindness. Psalm 63:3 tells us His lovingkindness is better than life itself: "Because Your lovingkindness is better than life, My lips shall praise You." I take this to mean that when I experience God's care, kindness and love, it is the exhilarating, comforting touch from Him that brings me life. There is nothing like it.

> We must keep our hearts and minds alert to the reality of God's ever-present care for us. We do this through praying in tongues.

An awareness of this comes as we pray in tongues. God's passion for us begins to witness in our spirit, which brings us unimaginable comfort, assurance and confirmation of who we are before the Lord. He cares for you and me. This means that everything is okay, because His love for us is certain and rock solid. Wow, the power of tongues!

## Mercy Is Our Destiny

The other thing praying in tongues does is create in us an anticipation of the mercy of God. Jude 21 also says we are to be "looking for the mercy of our Lord Jesus Christ unto eternal life." As we pray in tongues, we look forward to the future for which God has destined us. The Holy Spirit working in us will awaken us to the awareness that mercy and eternal life are our destination.

Many people live their lives full of dread and uncertainty about their future. This is where the three Ds come from. Discouragement, depression and disillusionment are all the results of fearing the future. When the Holy Spirit testifies in us about the future as we pray in tongues, however, it brings us life, encouragement and great faith. God has not appointed us to wrath, but to obtain mercy, according to 1 Thessalonians 5:8–9:

> But let us who are of the day be sober, putting on the breast-plate of faith and love, and as a helmet the hope of salvation. For God did not appoint us to wrath, but to obtain salvation through our Lord Jesus Christ.

Notice that we are to put on the *helmet* of salvation. This is spiritual attire that protects our minds and combats every fear that would seek to affect us. This helmet allows us to think correctly and realize that our portion is not wrath and judgment, but rather mercy and salvation. One of the main ways this helmet is set in place on us is through our praying in tongues in the Holy Spirit. Tongues cause us to be looking for the mercy and eternal life we have in Jesus. Instead of anticipating wrath, we are looking for God's mercy to be revealed. Instead of thinking judgment is coming, we expect His kindness and goodness.

The operation of tongues sets this helmet firmly in place, which guards our hearts and minds and makes us think clearly, soberly and righteously. While others around us are filled with dread, we are filled with faith and confidence as we pray in tongues and fellowship with the Lord on a deep level. As we pray in tongues and connect with the Lord on this deeper level, the Holy Spirit bears witness with our spirit that we are His.

## Assurance for Us All

This assurance is available to us all. When the Holy Spirit lives in us and we use the gift of tongues, which is so closely associated with His presence, God reveals Himself to us. In John 14:15–18, Jesus tells His disciples a mystery about how the Holy Spirit will reveal Himself to them, even while the world does not see Him:

> If you love Me, keep My commandments. And I will pray the Father, and He will give you another Helper, that He may abide with you forever—the Spirit of truth, whom the world cannot receive, because it neither sees Him nor knows Him; but you know Him, for He dwells with you and will be in you. I will not leave you orphans; I will come to you.

Jesus promises that the Spirit of truth will come and not only dwell with His disciples, but *in* them. This is the way that His disciples will have access to what everyone else is missing.

The world does not know or receive the Holy Spirit, yet as Jesus' disciples, we have entrance into what the rest of the world is missing. The Holy Spirit will manifest the Father and the Son to us, because we are not *orphans* who are left alone. We will experience the closeness of God through the Holy Spirit, and this confirming presence of the Lord will be our constant companion.

This sense of God's presence is inaugurated through the gift of tongues. As we pray in tongues, the closeness of who Jesus is comes to us. Every fear is vanquished, and trouble's every effect on us is subdued. The life, power and person of Jesus is near as we commune with God through the avenue of tongues. What an amazing gift God has made available to us. The three Ds are no match for the closeness of Jesus revealed to us through the ministry of the Holy Spirit and the gift of tongues.

# *Ten*

# MYSTERIES UNVEILED

I mentioned already that the gift of tongues helps unveil hidden mysteries of the spirit world. Again, we know this is true because of what 1 Corinthians 14:2 tells us: "For he who speaks in a tongue does not speak to men but to God, for no one understands him; however, in the spirit he speaks mysteries." When the Bible says those speaking in tongues are speaking mysteries, the implications go beyond just words that cannot be understood in the natural. The Greek word for *mysteries* is *musterion*, which means "to shut the mouth," "a secret" and "the idea of silence imposed by initiation into a religious circle." Paul is declaring that praying in tongues allows us *initiation* into a place in the spirit world where secrets are unveiled.

Tongues are languages that the spirit world responds to. When I pray in tongues, a door opens for me in the spirit that allows me entrance into places where mysteries are revealed. When I speak of a door, I am speaking of an access point that is unseen, yet real, into the spirit dimension.

It seems this is what Paul was directly or indirectly alluding to in 1 Corinthians 14:15, when he speaks of praying and singing *first* in the spirit, and *then* with his understanding: "What is the conclusion then? I will pray with the spirit, and I will also pray with the understanding. I will sing with the spirit, and I will also sing with the understanding." The order he is using, it would seem, is important. As Paul spoke and sang in tongues, it brought enlightenment to his understanding.

*When I pray in tongues, a door opens for me in the spirit that allows me entrance into places where mysteries are revealed.*

This is very consistent with my experience. God has used my praying in tongues to bring me revelation. As I pray in tongues, perhaps a Scripture is brought to my attention. Or maybe I am already thinking about a Scripture as I pray in tongues, and suddenly the meaning of it, along with new ideas about it that I have never thought of before, begin to form in my mind. People have asked me consistently through the years where and how I got the revelation I teach. I can say unequivocally that so much of it has come through praying in tongues, as I have just described.

As I pray in tongues, ideas and thoughts come. Fresh language and new terms materialize in my mind, which I can use as a means to communicate to others what I am understanding in the spirit. This is my understanding of being enlightened as I pray and/or sing in the spirit. Mysteries are unveiled in the spiritual dimension that I have been allowed to enter. My prayer language grants me access into a place of revelation.

## Two Worlds at One Time

It might be helpful to gain more of an understanding of what I mean by *dimensions of the spirit*, or as I have referred to it in previous chapters, the *spirit world*. Even though we live in a physical body in a physical world, we also are spiritual beings. We are actually made to live in two worlds at one time. This is what made Jesus so powerful. Even though He walked the earth as a mortal man, He was in constant contact with His Father in the unseen realm. John 5:19 helps reveal this, where Jesus is describing how He does miracles: "Most assuredly, I say to you, the Son can do nothing of Himself, but what He sees the Father do; for whatever He does, the Son also does in like manner."

Jesus claimed that He had no power of Himself to do miracles. He had laid aside His God powers when He came to earth, and He functioned here completely as a mortal man. Philippians 2:5–10 gives us more insight into this:

> Let this mind be in you which was also in Christ Jesus, who, being in the form of God, did not consider it robbery to be equal with God, but made Himself of no reputation, taking the form of a bondservant, and coming in the likeness of men. And being found in appearance as a man, He humbled Himself and became obedient to the point of death, even the death of the cross. Therefore God also has highly exalted Him and given Him the name which is above every name, that at the name of Jesus every knee should bow, of those in heaven, and of those on earth, and of those under the earth.

As a result of Jesus' absolute obedience and willingness to divest Himself of His God powers and live within human limitations, God the Father highly exalted Him. My main point, however, is that rather than functioning in His God powers, Jesus lived as a man *filled with God*.

This is the way we must function as well. We are not God, but we can be *filled with God* and manifest His glory. This is why John 14:12 makes the claim that we can and will do even greater works than Jesus did in His earthly ministry: "Most assuredly, I say to you, he who believes in Me, the works that I do he will do also; and greater works than these he will do, because I go to My Father." Jesus could make this statement because He did not operate as God while on the earth. He operated as a man filled with God through the Holy Spirit. The same power Jesus exhibited is the power we can walk in today because it operates through the ministry of the Holy Spirit, whom Jesus was filled with when He was baptized in Luke 3:21–22:

> When all the people were baptized, it came to pass that Jesus also was baptized; and while He prayed, the heaven was opened. And the Holy Spirit descended in bodily form like a dove upon Him, and a voice came from heaven which said, "You are My beloved Son; in You I am well pleased."

This occurrence was not simply something symbolic. Jesus actually was empowered with the Holy Spirit, just as we are. He had to have this power of the Spirit because He was not going to use His power as God. If He was to win back the human race from sin, He had to do it as a man. A man had lost it, and a man had to win it back. Otherwise, the devil would have had a legal case against God and could have accused Him of operating unlawfully. When Jesus functioned completely and solely as a man, however, the enemy's argument was lost.

This is all necessary for us to understand because Jesus lived as a man, functioned as a man, did miracles as a man and related to the Father as a man. This is why Jesus said that He could do nothing of Himself, except what He saw the Father do. He was totally dependent on perceiving what His Father was doing, and then moving in agreement with it. This is what allowed the supernatural and the miracles to happen.

This was all possible because Jesus not only lived as a human being in the natural; He also functioned simultaneously in the unseen realm of the spiritual dimension. He lived in two worlds at one time. From His relationship with His Father, He knew how to be aware of not only what was happening in the natural world, but also what was going on in the spirit world. Whatever He perceived in the unseen place from the Father, He agreed with it in the seen place, and it would happen.

This defends the idea that Jesus only functioned as a man while on the earth, although He was and is indeed God. As a man, He knew how to *see* what was happening in the invisible dimension. We are called to do the same. When we pray in tongues, we are granted access into these invisible places, which is why revelation comes. As we speak in tongues, pray and minister to the Lord, we are able to live in two dimensions, or worlds, at one time. Operating in tongues is an irrefutable necessity for us if we are to function as Jesus did. Tongues open the spirit world to us so we can behold mysteries in that unseen realm.

## Stewarding the Mysteries

We should understand what the Bible is saying or implying when it uses the term *mystery* or *mysteries*. Jesus used these words when He spoke to His disciples. In Matthew 13:10–11, He let the disciples know that certain things would be revealed to them that would remain hidden from those who were not hungry for God:

> And the disciples came and said to Him, "Why do You speak to them in parables?"
>
> He answered and said to them, "Because it has been given to you to know the mysteries of the kingdom of heaven, but to them it has not been given."

The disciples seemed puzzled over why Jesus would veil deep spiritual truth in stories, rather than just telling the people. Jesus explained that it was because *mysteries* are only revealed to those who hunger and thirst for Him and desire the Kingdom of God. The disciples had this virtue about them. The multitudes, on the other hand, only wanted what Jesus could do for them.

The principle concerning mysteries is basically this: Mysteries are only revealed to those who long for God. When we pray in tongues, if our tongues reveal a cry for God in us, then we will see revelations of God's mysteries. The yearning of our heart to find and know Him will result in mysteries being made known to us. God will trust us with precious things.

> *The principle concerning mysteries is basically this: Mysteries are only revealed to those who long for God.*

Deuteronomy 29:29 says God has secrets He will reveal: "The secret things belong to the LORD our God, but those things which are revealed belong to us and to our children forever, that we may do all the words of this law." When God reveals His secrets, we are then responsible for them. We have to take action concerning them, aligning our lives with them and beginning to walk in them. God will only unveil His secrets to those who hunger for Him and desire to obey Him.

There are those whom God will commission to steward His mysteries. In 1 Corinthians 4:1, Paul says that he and the other apostles were honored as those servants of Christ who stewarded the mysteries of God: "Let a man so consider us, as servants of Christ and stewards of the mysteries of God." The Lord designates the ones who are given the task of stewarding and handling the mysteries of God, because He has found them faithful to administer these mysteries to others. As Paul says in verse 2, "Moreover it is required in stewards that one be found faithful." The Lord regarded Paul and his apostolic company as faithful.

It would seem safe to project that many of the mysteries Paul stewarded came as a result of his praying in tongues. Paul revealed in 1 Corinthians 14:18–19 how much he prayed in tongues in his personal life:

> I thank my God I speak with tongues more than you all; yet in the church I would rather speak five words with my understanding, that I may teach others also, than ten thousand words in a tongue.

What a significant statement. Paul said that he prayed in tongues *more than* everyone combined. Clearly, his prayer life consisted of praying in tongues on a massive scale.

I remember that years ago, I was challenged to spend an hour a day in prayer. I knew this was what God was asking of me. When I began to set aside that hour, usually early in the morning, but sometimes at other times based on my schedule, it amazed me how *hard* it was to spend one hour straight through in prayer. I found that in the early days, I very quickly ran out of things to pray. I tried to worship. I found myself repeating the same thing over and over. I found my mind would wander. It seemed impossible to spend an hour in prayer and not get frustrated and quit. I would never have developed the prayer life I have today if it had not been for tongues. I knew that I could pray in tongues and begin to connect with the Lord Himself, and that is exactly what happened during that time. To this day, tongues are a huge part of my personal prayer time. I do pray in the spirit, and while I also pray with my understanding, as the Scripture says, praying in tongues constitutes a big part of my time before the Lord.

## Stepping into Revelation's Realm

Paul exercised this gift of tongues faithfully, more than anyone else. Yet in the Church, he wanted to speak in his natural language so other people might gain revelation. As I heard someone suggest years ago, "Could it be that Paul's exuberant amount of praying in tongues caused power to be in the five words he would speak in public?"

There is a connection between the two. When we pray in the spirit, we step into a realm where revelation is. We are then able to speak words of revelation under the anointing gleaned from being with Jesus. Five intelligible words produced from this place can affect, empower and change lives tremendously. The fact that Paul mentions only "five words" also reveals that the impact is not about the number of words spoken; it is about the *power* in those words.

*When we pray in the spirit, we step into a realm where revelation is. We are then able to speak words of revelation under the anointing gleaned from being with Jesus.*

May we spend time as stewards of the mysteries of God. As we commune and fellowship with the Lord, revelation will come that changes life on the planet. As we minister to the Lord in tongues, God can show us things that have been hidden. Literally, a mystery can be something that has never been known before, but now has reached the time for its unveiling. Romans 16:25 gives us insight into Paul bringing forth such mysteries:

Now to Him who is able to establish you according to my gospel and the preaching of Jesus Christ, according to the revelation of the mystery kept secret since the world began . . .

Think about this: Paul was allowed to understand a truth or idea that no one else had ever seen before. It had been kept secret since the world began. It was time, however, for the truth to be revealed in his day. There were many different aspects of it, but Paul revealed the mystery of *justification through faith*. He was the vessel God had chosen to show us this revelation, which would change the world and the way that we approach God. Since Paul was clear that praying in tongues was a speaking and revealing of mysteries, it would stand to reason that tongues were part of the process he went through to gain this revelation. Paul was bringing to light things that had up to that point been unknown as he prayed in tongues.

I believe there are some necessities for the Church's function and assignment that are yet to be unveiled. This means that we need to pray in tongues, as the Spirit grants us utterance. We need to allow this gift of tongues to unlock our understanding, showing forth hidden truths that will be required for what we have been called to do. I think this is probably what happened in Acts 13:1–3, where it seems as though the disciples simply began by worshiping, loving and ministering to the Lord:

> Now in the church that was at Antioch there were certain prophets and teachers: Barnabas, Simeon who was called Niger, Lucius of Cyrene, Manaen who had been brought up with Herod the tetrarch, and Saul. As they ministered to the Lord and fasted, the Holy Spirit said, "Now separate to Me Barnabas and Saul for the work to which I have called them." Then, having fasted and prayed, and laid hands on them, they sent them away.

These prophets and teachers got a revelation to send Barnabas and Saul forth. This changed the landscape and history of the Church. Could it be that as they prayed in tongues and worshiped the Lord corporately, this life-changing revelation came? I believe so.

Many times, when we pray in tongues, we are simply ministering to the Lord. We are just loving Him and delighting ourselves in Him. As the disciples were doing this, God spoke clearly, and everyone knew it. A mystery was unveiled out of ministering to the Lord, of which tongues were a part. The Lord showed them His secrets and unlocked their understanding. This is such a holy and pure thing before the Lord.

May we approach God with our ministry to Him in tongues. As we do this, the wells of our understanding can be unlocked. Psalm 25:14 says that as we fear the Lord and approach Him, He shows us His secrets: "The secret of the Lord is with those who fear Him, and He will show them His covenant." As we bless Him from the deepest part of our heart, He will unveil His wisdom to us. Maybe it will be about a Scripture. Perhaps it will be a key to success. Or it could be an unknown business idea that will unlock wealth. Whatever it is that comes, it is a mystery that God has determined it is time to reveal. May we approach the Lord through tongues and step into the realm of revelation, where the mysteries of God are made known.

*Eleven*

# GIVING THANKS

Worship and adoration of the Lord are part of what can happen as we pray in tongues. We also can be giving thanks for who God is and what He does. This can be a very high form of worship. It seems that the disciples were doing these things on the Day of Pentecost, when they spoke in tongues. We saw in Acts 2 that they were speaking in languages they had never learned naturally. They probably did not even know what they were saying; they were just honoring and worshiping God for how great He is. The bystanders who were listening exclaimed, "We hear them speaking in our own tongues the wonderful works of God" (verse 11). Without knowledge of what they were saying, the disciples were proclaiming God's mighty works, worshiping His awesomeness and declaring His kindness and goodness.

Tongues have a great place in our worship and thanksgiving. They bypass our mind and intellect and allow the Holy Spirit to move in us and through us. Remember that the Holy Spirit has

165

come to speak of Jesus, according to John 16:13–15. He has come to reveal who Jesus is:

> However, when He, the Spirit of truth, has come, He will guide you into all truth; for He will not speak on His own authority, but whatever He hears He will speak; and He will tell you things to come. He will glorify Me, for He will take of what is Mine and declare it to you. All things that the Father has are Mine. Therefore I said that He will take of Mine and declare it to you.

The Holy Spirit will take all that belongs to Jesus and reveal it to us. We also see that He will glorify the Lord Jesus. This is because salvation is only in Jesus and His name. The Holy Spirit will unveil and emphasize who Jesus is, because Jesus is the only way to the Father. Under the unction of the Holy Spirit, Peter declared in Acts 4:11–12 that only by believing in Jesus and His name can we be saved:

> This is the "stone which was rejected by you builders, which has become the chief cornerstone." Nor is there salvation in any other, for there is no other name under heaven given among men by which we must be saved.

Salvation only comes by believing in who Jesus is and what He has done. He is the only way.

John 14:6 gives us Jesus' historic statement: "I am the way, the truth, and the life. No one comes to the Father except through Me." Jesus' claim is that only through Him can we have salvation, and only through Him will the Father receive us. As a result of this, when the Holy Spirit came to the earth, His commissioning as the third part of the Trinity was to glorify Jesus. Through the Spirit's activity and conviction, people are brought to an awareness of who Jesus is and their need for His saving power.

It is therefore no wonder that when we pray in tongues, through the Holy Spirit we can be glorifying Jesus. We are lifting Him up and magnifying who He is in the spirit realm. This worship and thanks can be very powerful. Our worship of Jesus in the spirit, through tongues inspired by the Holy Spirit, causes things to move in the unseen world. When we worship, we allow God to be enthroned in our lives and in the situations we face. Psalm 22:3 shows that as we worship and praise the Lord, we invite Him to rule over our lives: "But You are holy, enthroned in the praises of Israel." We invoke the presence of the Lord through our adoration.

*Our worship of Jesus in the spirit, through tongues inspired by the Holy Spirit, causes things to move in the unseen world. When we worship, we allow God to be enthroned in our lives and in the situations we face.*

Years ago, I heard a story from a friend of mine who had been called to minister in a nation where tribal culture was very prevalent. In such situations, if the chief of a tribe surrendered to the Lordship of Jesus, then usually the whole tribe would follow. The reverse was also true. If the chief resisted the claims of the Lord over his life and soul, then the people rejected Christ as well. In this kind of setting, my friend was invited to sit with a certain chief among his people. As he did, this chief and his people began to clap in a rhythmic cadence. As they clapped, two girls danced to the rhythm in the midst of everyone. In agreement with unseen demonic powers, the people continued to clap and chant, and the girls began to ascend upward. At the pinnacle of their ascent, they were hanging ten feet in the air, suspended by this invisible force.

The chief then looked at the minister and asked, "What can your God do?"

My friend replied to the chief, "My God can bring them down."

The chief gave my friend the go-ahead. As my friend rose and went to stand under the suspended girls, he did not rebuke the powers of darkness. He did not bind the wickedness or command these powers to be silenced. As he stood under these girls, he said he simply lifted his hands and began to worship the Lord. As he began to worship, the invisible force that was lifting up and holding these girls in midair clearly fled, and the girls came crashing to the ground.

My friend's worship of the Lord enthroned God over the situation. His worship had allowed God to arise and His enemies to flee, according to the Word of God (see Psalm 68:1). The result was a manifestation of God far more powerful than the powers of the devil, and as a result this whole tribe eventually came to know the Lord. The people became followers of Jesus and left behind their worship of demons. This is because my friend's simple act of worship shifted the unseen atmosphere. As we worship in our known language, but also especially in the language of the Holy Spirit, we can see the Lord lifted high and enthroned over all our lives and circumstances. He is indeed Lord of all.

## Making Our Song Personal

Ephesians 5:18–20 gives us a glimpse into the worship and thanks that can flow from us through *spiritual songs*:

> And do not be drunk with wine, in which is dissipation; but be filled with the Spirit, speaking to one another in psalms and hymns and spiritual songs, singing and making melody in your

heart to the Lord, giving thanks always for all things to God the Father in the name of our Lord Jesus Christ.

Notice that through these different expressions of worship, we are giving thanks to God as our Father. *Psalms* and *hymns* are most likely a reference to singing something in a known language. *Spiritual songs*, however, could easily be construed as worship flowing from the gift of tongues. Again, we know such songs can be a prevalent aspect of the Holy Spirit's movement in us through the gift of tongues. Remember that Paul himself said he would sing with the spirit, and with his understanding.

To gain a fuller understanding of worship and thanksgiving through tongues, we should have an appreciation for worship itself. Worship is not just what happens before the preacher or pastor preaches on Sunday morning. Worship is meant to be a critical part of our communion with the Lord. Through worship, we enter into a connection with Him. The root idea of worship is to declare someone's worth, which is what we do as we worship the Lord. We are proclaiming His worth to us and lifting Him up high above the normal realms of life. This can only occur out of a revelation of who He is. Real worship, at its core, has revelation in it. This is why in John 4:19–26, Jesus told the woman at the well that it takes an inspired understanding of who God is to truly worship:

> The woman said to Him, "Sir, I perceive that You are a prophet. Our fathers worshiped on this mountain, and you Jews say that in Jerusalem is the place where one ought to worship."
>
> Jesus said to her, "Woman, believe Me, the hour is coming when you will neither on this mountain, nor in Jerusalem, worship the Father. You worship what you do not know; we know what we worship, for salvation is of the Jews. But the hour is coming, and now is, when the true worshipers will worship

The Gift of Tongues

the Father in spirit and truth; for the Father is seeking such to worship Him. God is Spirit, and those who worship Him must worship in spirit and truth."

The woman said to Him, "I know that Messiah is coming" (who is called Christ). "When He comes, He will tell us all things."

Jesus said to her, "I who speak to you am He."

Jesus had previously told this woman that she had had five husbands and was now living with a man who was not her husband. She declared from this encounter that Jesus must be a prophet. Jesus had also told her that He could give her living water. Then the conversation shifted to worship. I personally believe that worship is essential to drinking from the living water. When we sing with our understanding, but also sing in the spirit through tongues, we begin to tap into these realms of the Spirit.

I remember when I was seeking to bring the first church where I was senior pastor into a deeper place of worship. The worship at that time was pretty dry and barren. On one particular Sunday morning, I did a message on singing in the spirit. I told the church that singing words off the pages of a book or an overhead screen is like giving a greeting card with a message the card company has printed in it. It is nice and kind, but it is not a real, personal touch. I then said that when we sing in the spirit, it is like the additional words that we write personally at the end of a greeting card's printed words. These words we add are usually the ones that mean the most to the person receiving it, because they are our own personal thoughts of love and care. As I concluded the message, I led the church in a song we all knew. As we finished the song, I then exhorted the people to begin to sing to the Lord in English—and also in the spirit—about their own personal love for Him. The very presence of God suddenly was among us as we did that, and we were very aware of it.

A very precious lady in the church told me later that when I was teaching, she thought that what I was saying was incorrect. Then when I had us all sing a known song, and then I encouraged everyone to sing their own song of love to the Lord, she said something happened. She told me, "Suddenly, what I was singing moved from here [she pointed to her head] to here [she pointed to her stomach]." She was expressing what I knew could happen from worship born of the Spirit of God. No longer were we worshiping out of our natural understanding; we had begun to worship from our spirit, under the unction of the Holy Spirit. The gift of tongues was a major part of this. As this woman sang in her prayer language, her love of the Lord and her devotion to Him flowed like a river through her. This can be that place of deep intimacy and life we experience as we worship with tongues in God's presence.

## Truths about Worship

When Jesus was speaking with the woman at the well, He unveiled several distinct truths about worship and partaking of the living water that can flow through us by His Holy Spirit. We have seen that this flow can be released quite powerfully through tongues. Jesus knew this woman was searching, so part of His discourse with her was aimed at unlocking real, true worship from the depths of her being. That unquenchable thirst inside her would then be filled by the power of the Holy Spirit.

The first truth about worship Jesus spoke to this woman is that it is not about a *location*. He told her it was not about worshiping on this mountain or at that place. Real worship is worshiping an unseen God from the spirit. This means we don't need all the trappings of today to worship adequately, because worship is something that flows from our inner person. If we *need* the instruments, the singers, the smoke machines, the right lighting and other artificial inclinations to worship, then maybe we have not truly discovered real worship. We might be having more of an emotional response than a spiritual one. True, unadulterated worship flows from a sincere heart reaching out to the living God. This cry of the heart will never be denied.

> *True, unadulterated worship flows from a sincere heart reaching out to the living God. This cry of the heart will never be denied.*

A second truth about worship Jesus unveiled to this woman is that it requires *revelation*. I have already mentioned that the Holy Spirit shows the glory of who Jesus and the Father are, so that we might worship. When by the Spirit we behold their majesty, we are compelled to worship. Jesus told her salvation belongs to the Jews, and therefore they worship from revelation. This would mean that only by revelation of who the Lord is can we really be saved.

At the time Jesus said this, He had only been sent to the lost sheep of Israel (see Matthew 15:24). The time of the Gentiles had not yet come. This was why He said that salvation was for the Jews. As a result of this, the Holy Spirit was available to show the Jews who Jesus really was, that He might be worshiped. Today, however, we are grafted in as Gentile believers (see Romans 11:17–18). The Holy Spirit is therefore showing us who Jesus is. From this revelation, worship should flow out of us that adores the Father and the Son. Part of this flow comes through the gift of tongues. We can worship with a pure stream of love for the Lord, as in the Holy Spirit we behold God's beauty.

David spoke of God's beauty in Psalm 27:4: "One thing I have desired of the LORD, that will I seek: That I may dwell in the house of the LORD all the days of my life, to behold the beauty of the LORD, and to inquire in His temple." The cry of David's heart was to *behold the beauty of the Lord*. When this is our heart cry, it causes worship to manifest in and through us. Tongues can give a pure release to this that perhaps natural language cannot. We begin to worship in a depth of spirit that connects to our empowerment in God. He helps the river to flow through us, which involves tongues, as we worship from the revelation of who He is.

A third truth about worship Jesus showed this woman was that God is *seeking worshipers*. Notice that God does not seek worship; He seeks worshipers. The Lord is not insecure in who He is. He does not need for us to stroke Him and tell Him how great He is. Worship is actually much more for us than it is for Him. When we worship out of a revelation of who God is, it changes us. As we behold Him in worship, the fabric of who we are is changed. As we partake of His graciousness through His closeness and presence, we are made gracious. The grace of who He is begins to penetrate the core of our being.

The principle is that whatever we worship, we become like. Psalm 115:3–8 shows that those who worship idols become like what they worship:

> But our God is in heaven; He does whatever He pleases. Their idols are silver and gold, the work of men's hands. They have mouths, but they do not speak; eyes they have, but they do not see; they have ears, but they do not hear; noses they have, but they do not smell; they have hands, but they do not handle; feet they have, but they do not walk; nor do they mutter through their throat. Those who make them are like them; so is everyone who trusts in them.

This describes the dumb, speechless, powerless idols that men worshiped, and the passage ends with the declaration that *those who make them are like them.* But if we worship the Lord, we become like Him, for we behold Him as He is. This is the principle that worship has the power to fashion us into the image of what we are worshiping. When we worship in spirit and in truth through tongues, the power to change is enacted in us. We are transformed into the image of the firstborn Son of God. This is why the Lord is seeking worshipers. It is the power of the Holy Spirit released in us that changes us from glory to glory.

The final truth I will mention that Jesus was sharing with this thirsty woman is that our worship experience should be a *progressive* thing. He told her that "the hour is coming, and now is, when the true worshipers will worship the Father in spirit and truth" (John 4:23). The phrase "the hour is coming, and now is" indicates that a revelation we have that is producing worship will have an ongoing, ever-increasing expression to it. In other words, our worship will enlarge and change continually as we worship in spirit and truth.

> *Our natural languages have boundaries and limits that tongues do not have. Through tongues, our expression of worship will continue to grow and flow.*

There are many different expressions of worship, and we will have many different experiences as we engage in it. This is especially true when the gift of tongues is involved. Our natural languages have boundaries and limits that tongues do not have. Through tongues, our expression of worship will continue to grow and flow. As we worship in spirit and truth, the expression flowing from us can go deeper and deeper, as we discover a reservoir in God that is unlocked through the gift of tongues.

May we, through the gift of tongues, give thanks well. May we learn to allow the flow of the Holy Spirit to so declare the greatness of God that we drink deeply of the living water as the Spirit moves through us in divine and acceptable worship. God will be glorified in this, and we will be changed!

## Twelve

# THE INTERPRETATION
# OF TONGUES

W hen we consider tongues and their operation, we must look at the idea of the interpretation of these tongues. Through the interpretation of tongues, the mysteries we speak can be made known and shared. Remember that when we speak in a tongue, we are speaking mysteries. These are secrets that have been hidden, which God now desires to unveil. Through the interpretation of tongues, we can see this done. Tongues by themselves can bring great blessing to us as individuals. When they are coupled with interpretation, however, great blessing and empowerment can come to the Church, the Body of Christ, as well as to us individually.

Through the interpretation of tongues, we can realize *what* we are saying in our own prayer language. This is why Paul used the order of praying and singing in the spirit, and then praying and singing with understanding (see again 1 Corinthians 14:15). The idea is that as we pray and sing in tongues, and then are granted the interpretation, we can go on to pray and sing with our understanding the mysteries that we have just spoken in tongues.

This process requires the interpretation of tongues, which is available for any and all of us to function in as we pray in tongues. This is what makes the gift of tongues so powerful. Since my natural mind is unoccupied when I speak in tongues, it follows that I can "listen" at the same time. In the natural, it is difficult to listen at the same time as I am speaking or praying in my normal language, because both activities engage my mind. But when I pray in tongues, I am praying in the spirit, but I can also be listening for the interpretation. This is when the mysteries I have been speaking can be unlocked and unveiled.

## Interpretation Is Not Translation

One of the key factors to realize about all this is that the Bible speaks of tongues being *interpreted* and not necessarily *translated*. We are admonished in 1 Corinthians 14:13 that if we speak in tongues, we should also pray to be able to interpret them: "Therefore let him who speaks in a tongue pray that he may interpret." That is different from *translation*, however, which is a verbatim, word-for-word version of something that is spoken, meaning it is literal or exact. *Interpretation* can be the explanation of a thought or idea. So when a tongue is interpreted, it does not mean that it is a word-for-word translation; it means that the idea of what is being spoken is revealed.

I have spoken many times internationally through translators, and I have noticed that as they translate what I speak, sometimes the length of their translation seems much longer than what I originally said. When I ask about it, the translators explain that they are unveiling the thoughts and ideas I am speaking about, not just my literal words. Their answer actually gives us a much better understanding of what happens when tongues are interpreted. An interpretation is the idea, revelation or mystery being made known, rather than the exact, literal words being spoken. The interpretation is the thought being communicated in tongues, not necessarily a word-for-word explanation of every syllable.

*When a tongue is interpreted, it does not mean that it is a word-for-word translation; it means that the idea of what is being spoken is revealed.*

So as I pray in tongues, thoughts may began to emerge in my spirit and mind. Quite often, these thoughts are mysteries being made known as a result of praying in tongues. This interpretation provides an idea of what the Holy Spirit is revealing as I pray in tongues. My example here takes place on an individual level, but it also manifests this same way in a corporate setting. Paul addressed this in 1 Corinthians 14, where he made some significant observations and gave specific instructions to the Corinthian church (and to us) about the operation of these gifts. In verses 1–5, he said that any use of the spiritual gifts in a corporate setting should be done to edify the Church:

> Pursue love, and desire spiritual gifts, but especially that you may prophesy. For he who speaks in a tongue does not speak to men but to God, for no one understands him; however, in the spirit he speaks mysteries. But he who prophesies speaks edification and exhortation and comfort to men. He who speaks in a tongue edifies himself, but he who prophesies edifies the church. I wish you all spoke with tongues, but even more that you prophesied; for he who prophesies is greater than he who speaks with tongues, unless indeed he interprets, that the church may receive edification.

All expressions of the Holy Spirit's gifts are to be used to build up and strengthen the Church and the people connected to it as individuals. This includes tongues. Tongues in the Church are therefore to be interpreted. Paul goes so far as to say that it is better to prophesy and bring edification, exhortation and comfort while in a corporate gathering than it is to speak in a tongue that no one understands—unless the tongue is interpreted. Interpretation allows people to understand what is being said, and they are then encouraged and empowered.

## Tongues Speak to God

Traditionally speaking, it has been thought and taught that this passage we just read from Paul is talking about a *message from God* coming forth in tongues. In other words, that one person will speak out, and another will interpret, whatever God is saying to the Church. This actually goes against what Paul says as he addresses this whole issue. He clearly says that when someone speaks in tongues, the person is *speaking to God and not man*. This would mean that the gift of tongues is not the other way around, a *message to man from God*. Tongues are worship, adoration and prayer from us *to God*.

If this is correct, which it is since we receive no different instruction anywhere else in Scripture, then when tongues are expressed in a corporate gathering, they express *a prayer to God, not a message to us*. Tongues therefore should be interpreted as such.

My contention is that if tongues and interpretation are the equivalent of prophecy, then they are redundant. There is no real or different benefit. If, however, tongues and interpretation are prayer and worship offered to God through the power of the Holy Spirit, then this is a great advantage. Plus, it agrees with Scripture and does not make up a new set of rules unseen in the Bible.

Some might ask, "Why, then, have we seen people speak in tongues in a service, and then seen a message from God be delivered when there's an interpretation?"

The answer is really quite simple. This happens because of the way we have been taught. If we think tongues and interpretation bring a message *from God to people*, then that is the way they are addressed and spoken forth. But remember, interpretation does not mean giving a word-for-word translation. To interpret is to provide the sense of the thought or idea that is being expressed. If we have had the correct teaching that *tongues speak to God*, then we will

> *When tongues are expressed in a corporate gathering, they express a prayer to God, not a message to us. Tongues therefore should be interpreted as such.*

interpret and speak forth the ideas behind them, the things being made known to us in the spirit realm, in this way.

For instance, if a tongue is spoken in a corporate gathering and the interpretation comes out of the old mindset that God is speaking *to us*, the interpretation might sound like this: "'I love you,' says the Lord. . . ." If, however, the interpretation comes out of the right mindset of tongues being our expressions *to God*, this would change. The interpretation might become, "Thank You so much, Lord, for how much You love us. . . ." The interpretation becomes a statement of prayer and praise to the Lord, rather than a statement from God to us.

We are always a product of the way we have been taught. As our understanding changes about what the gift of tongues is, then our operation in tongues will change as well. We will no longer be repeating what prophecy is, which is God speaking to us, but will in fact see a different and unique expression of the Holy Spirit operating among us in the form of tongues. The Church will be edified as, through the revelation of who God is, we experience a new level of worship, perhaps intercession, and adoration through the gift of tongues and interpretation. Who knows what might be expressed? The only limits that would be upon us are the limits of the Holy Spirit, and here is the wonderful news: He has no limits! As we allow His glorious presence to move in us and through us, who knows what might flow in our midst?

## Varieties of Tongues

One other thought about tongues and interpretation is that as they operate on a corporate level, the Bible refers to them as *different kinds of tongues*, or *varieties of tongues*. First Corinthians 12 communicates this idea in two places. Verse 10 lists "different kinds of tongues" as part of the nine gifts in which the Holy Spirit might operate in a church setting. We also see this gifting listed in verse 28, which sets it in a significant place in the operation of a local assembly: "And God has appointed these in the church: first apostles, second prophets, third teachers, after that miracles, then gifts of healings, helps, administrations, varieties of tongues." Out of everything the apostle Paul could have listed here, he included varieties of tongues.

The words *different kinds* and *varieties* in these verses are actually the same word in the Greek, *genos*. It means "to cause to be, to generate," "something born" or "to be kin." *Genos* therefore means things that are related, or of the same group. I have seen this variety of tongues happen both in my private life and in a public/corporate gathering. There have been times when my prayer language *dialect* has changed, and I have been aware of a slight adjustment in the sound, words and inflection being expressed. As I look back, I can see that this was probably connected to a new assignment being given to me, a new mantle being released or a new season of life and ministry beginning. In different instances, I began to function in a new *kind* of tongue. It would seem that the different tongue was part of stepping into and even pioneering the new dimension being granted me.

From what Paul says, it would appear that not only does God use apostles, prophets, teachers and other significant ministries, but He also works through *varieties of tongues*. The inclusion of various tongues in this list would seem to declare that those who speak in tongues in a corporate gathering are essential and significant. They are able to speak under the influence of the Holy Spirit in different expressions and dialects. These various tongues would then require interpretation, as mandated by Paul.

There must be a reason for these different kinds or varieties of tongues. God has designed them to do different things in the spirit world as they are released. Different words have different effects upon different cultures. We have to trust this all to God and just move by faith. It seems ludicrous that God would do something for no reason, so we can be sure that the various tongues are of significance in the scheme of His purpose and plan.

> God has designed different kinds or varieties of tongues to do different things in the spirit world as they are released. Different words have different effects upon different cultures.

Many years ago, as I was in training for ministry, we were in a midweek service. Our pastor had brought an outstanding teaching, as usual. He had us stand at the end of the service and just begin to worship. I had never spoken out in tongues in a service before, although I had prophesied many times. Speaking in tongues in a service setting was not something I did. As we were in this place of worship, I could *feel* the movement of the Holy Spirit stirring in me, and I felt I was to speak out in tongues. I wrestled with this for a few moments, not wanting to be improper or out of order. I finally concluded that it was what I should do. I opened my mouth and began to speak.

I expected my normal prayer language to come out of my mouth in that moment. Instead, a completely different dialect of tongues rolled out of me. It was a variety of tongues, different and yet very akin to my normal tongue. As it came forth, someone else interpreted it. Everyone seemed blessed by it.

As Mary and I got in the car to go home afterward, I asked her, "Did the tongue I spoke out sound different?" I was quite sure it had, but I wanted to get confirmation.

"Yes," Mary said, "it was different from what I normally hear you pray."

That settled it. I knew that as I had spoken, the tongue had not only *sounded* different; it had also *felt* different. I did not know then, nor do I know now, all that was happening in that moment. Somehow or other, though, that tongue was released through me and was stirring things in the spirit realm.

The fact that I remember 35-plus years later this one instance of a different tongue tells you how much of an impact it had. We must make room for different kinds of tongues, the interpretation of those tongues and the effects they are meant to have on the Church. These various tongues are a tool of God and of the Holy Spirit, used to shift things in the spirit world so that God's will is done.

# *Thirteen*

# PROPER PROTOCOL

When we consider the operation of tongues and interpretation in the Church, there are certain protocols that apply. There are at least five distinct things we should be aware of as tongues and interpretation take place in a corporate gathering. These five protocols will cause these gifts to be beneficial in the operation of the Church and in God's purposes working through it.

These five important protocols include *edifying the Church*, *bringing confirmation (not confusion)*, *taking turns*, *keeping silent at times* and *knowing there is divine order*. Observing proper protocol in the operation of the Holy Spirit's gifts enables us to become an empowered and healthy people for the Lord to work through as His Body. Let's look at each of these protocols in more detail.

## Protocol 1: Edifying the Church

The first protocol for us to observe is that everything should be done for the edification of the Church, meaning that the

Church is built up spiritually and numerically. Through these gifts in operation, people become empowered to make an overall contribution to the Church and its divine mission. This is why Paul says in Ephesians 4:14–16 that we are to grow up in Christ, as every part does its share:

> We should no longer be children . . . but, speaking the truth in love, may grow up in all things into Him who is the head— Christ—from whom the whole body, joined and knit together by what every joint supplies, according to the effective working by which every part does its share, causes growth of the body for the edifying of itself in love.

When every part does its share and every joint supplies what it is designed to supply, the Church grows. This is the Lord's ultimate intent. Church growth is not supposed to be about a talented, gifted person on a platform. Church growth is supposed to be the result of Body life. Everything we do as individual parts of the Body should be designed to make the Church grow. This means spiritual growth, but also numerical growth as people are saved and added to the Church regularly.

*When every part does its share and every joint supplies what it is designed to supply, the Church grows. This is the Lord's ultimate intent.*

Notice also that the Body of Christ edifies itself in love, according to this passage. The Church is put together in such a way that the love of God flows through its connections. The result is a healed, healthy expression in the Body of who Jesus is in the earth. This is the picture Ephesians 1:22–23 paints of the Church being the fullness of Jesus that fills all in all: "And He put all things under His feet, and gave Him to be head over all things to the

church, which is His body, the fullness of Him who fills all in all."
We as the Church are to be so built up, encouraged, strengthened
and edified that we will manifest the fullness of who Jesus is.

Over and over in 1 Corinthians 14, we see Paul exhorting us
that the building up and affirming of the Church is the main
reason for the gifts of the Spirit, including tongues. Let's look
one more time at 1 Corinthians 14:4–5, where Paul presses believers to operate in prophecy, tongues and interpretation for
the edifying of the Church:

> He who speaks in a tongue edifies himself, but he who proph-
> esies edifies the church. I wish you all spoke with tongues, but
> even more that you prophesied; for he who prophesies is greater
> than he who speaks with tongues, unless indeed he interprets,
> that the church may receive edification.

Through tongues and interpretation, the Church is strengthened. In a churchwide setting, these gifts operate so that the
corporate Body of the Church is made strong. This means the
gifts pull us together into a unity and power that we can only
gain as a mature expression of God's people.

Any gift in operation should bring unity and not division. It
should cause harmony to arise and not division to occur. This
way, the Church is built up and empowered. First Corinthians
14:12–13 also echoes this challenge to use the gifts of the Holy
Spirit and tongues to edify the Church: "Even so you, since you
are zealous for spiritual gifts, let it be for the edification of the
church that you seek to excel. Therefore let him who speaks in
a tongue pray that he may interpret." The apostle Paul did not
discourage people from desiring spiritual gifts and expressions,
but he did say they should want them for the right reasons. The
gifts are not given to make someone famous or develop a following for that person. The gifts are designed to edify the Church.

The gifts allow Jesus to love His Church through the power of the Holy Spirit moving through us. Jesus loves His Bride, His Body, His Church, and He uses the gifts of the Holy Spirit to minister to and strengthen it. Paul's exhortation was that we know and recognize why the gifts operate. They are not employed out of selfish ambition, but from a place of love. In 1 Corinthians 13:1–2, Paul addresses what happens when tongues and prophecy operate without love. In this passage, he clearly defines how love for God and His people must be the foundation we stand on as we move in the gifts and in faith:

> Though I speak with the tongues of men and of angels, but have not love, I have become sounding brass or a clanging cymbal. And though I have the gift of prophecy, and understand all mysteries and all knowledge, and though I have all faith, so that I could remove mountains, but have not love, I am nothing.

Without love as the motivating factor, our use of the Holy Spirit's gifts will just be noise. Even if I could do amazing exploits, if they were not done for the benefit of the Church and building it up, they would have no value. Because we want to see the Church built up and strengthened, tongues spoken out in a church setting should always be interpreted, as we talked about in the previous chapter. The interpretation brings power and might to the Church.

In 1 Corinthians 14:26, Paul gives us another exhortation to use the gifts to empower the overall Church: "How is it then, brethren? Whenever you come together, each of you has a psalm, has a teaching, has a tongue, has a revelation, has an interpretation. Let all things be done for edification." Paul again emphasizes here that the Church is to be our focus when it comes to using tongues and the other gifts. Our prayer should be that the gifts would flow through us and would be used not to build us a ministry personally, but to build the Church itself. This must be our focus on the corporate level.

## Protocol 2: Bringing Confirmation

A second protocol to observe in the operation of tongues and interpretation is always to let them *bring confirmation (not confusion)*. It would seem from Paul's writings that in the Corinthian church, their services were a free-for-all. Paul's description of what should *not* be done with tongues gives us some insight into what was happening. They must have been speaking forth tongues with no interpretation. In 1 Corinthians 14:7–11, Paul speaks of people not feeling confirmation as a result, but rather being confused:

> Even things without life, whether flute or harp, when they make a sound, unless they make a distinction in the sounds, how will it be known what is piped or played? For if the trumpet makes an uncertain sound, who will prepare for battle? So likewise you, unless you utter by the tongue words easy to understand, how will it be known what is spoken? For you will be speaking into the air. There are, it may be, so many kinds of languages in the world, and none of them is without significance. Therefore, if I do not know the meaning of the language, I shall be a foreigner to him who speaks, and he who speaks will be a foreigner to me.

Tongues without interpretation in the local assembly make people feel uncertain. They can be left wondering, *Do we prepare for battle, or not? Is this piped or played?* (Meaning that the distinction of a sound could be unclear.) *What is really being spoken?* Uninterpreted, the words have no real impact because they are just going forth into the air. It is as if I am listening to a foreigner speaking. The speaker may have great passion, but I don't know what is being said.

189

This seems to be what was happening in the Corinthian church. Paul never said that the tongues and gifts in evidence there were not the real thing in operation. He just said that they were bringing more confusion than confirmation. Every operation of the gifts must produce a confirming and life-giving result.

In 1 Corinthians 14:23, Paul also addresses the result of ministering in the gifts without proper wisdom and protocol: "Therefore if the whole church comes together in one place, and all speak with tongues, and there come in those who are uninformed or unbelievers, will they not say that you are out of your mind?" Paul is pressing the Church always to use tongues with interpretation. Without interpretation following in response to tongues, people will say we are mad and crazy. With proper use of tongues and interpretation, however, the impact will be great. Tongues with interpretation produce a confirmation of the Church and its people.

It can be quite amazing when people see the demonstration of tongues and interpretation. If the operation of these gifts is done correctly, people can become intrigued. It gains their interest, and they are even built up and empowered as a result. I was in a service where lost people were present, as well as people who were saved but did not understand the Spirit-filled life. Suddenly someone spoke in tongues, and another person interpreted. I was so concerned with what these outsiders and the uninformed would think. I told myself, "*Well, there they go. They'll never come back, even if they last through the service.*"

> *It can be quite amazing when people see the demonstration of tongues and interpretation. If the operation of these gifts is done correctly, people can become intrigued.*

When the service was over, I was amazed that these people were still there. One even said to me, "That was really something, the way those people did things right on cue."

I asked, "What are you talking about?"

The person then described the tongues and interpretation, which flowed so seamlessly that this outsider actually thought these gifts were a planned and practiced part of the service. In other words, this person thought the gifts were scripted. I had to explain what had really happened. When I did, the outsider was not offended at all, but was actually intrigued and amazed.

Many times, I think we limit what God can do, because we are thinking it will offend people. In reality, if we would allow Jesus to be the Head of the Church and move among us through the Holy Spirit, people would be touched. I am convinced that we need to trust God more and allow Him to be Lord in our midst.

## Protocol 3: Taking Turns

The third protocol for operating in tongues and interpretation is that each one should have a share, or *take turns*. In 1 Corinthians 14:27, Paul tells the Church how to use tongues in a divine order: "If anyone speaks in a tongue, let there be two or at the most three, each in turn, and let one interpret." I believe that in the operation of tongues in an assembly, this means up to three people could speak in tongues, and then one would interpret the essence of what all three have said. This would mean that all three tongues would carry the same idea and/or ideas connected one to the other. Under the leadership of the Holy Spirit, the words, prayer, adoration and other potential expressions are spoken forth, and then someone interprets them all. This arrangement was designed to keep order and confusion out so that the Church could benefit from the unction in operation.

When we read these instructions, it is clear that Paul is bringing order to this scenario. He is giving these practical tactics for the operation of tongues and interpretation to help the Corinthian church (and us) not diminish the use of the gifts, but rather see them become even more beneficial.

As a leader in the Body of Christ, I have been accused more than a few times of "quenching the Holy Spirit." If those people had really known my heart, they would never have said such a thing. My passion is for the manifestation of the Spirit of God among His people. I believe it will take the power of the Spirit to change a person's life, and also to change the culture we live in. Yet wisdom is necessary as we seek to unleash the Spirit of God among us.

"Do not quench the Spirit," Paul says in 1 Thessalonians 5:19. We spoke in some detail in chapter 2 about this idea of quenching the Spirit. It is one of the sins against the Holy Spirit, and it involves the idea of putting a fire out and not allowing it to burn rampantly. We must make room for the Holy Spirit to move. Yet Paul does place some guidelines, or protocols, in place for the operation of the Holy Spirit's gifts in the Church. This was not to stifle His movement, but to strengthen the positive effect of the Holy Spirit among the people. Many would have accused Paul of quenching the Spirit, yet Paul's purpose was not to clamp down on the Holy Spirit and His impact, but rather to allow Him to produce greater positive results. This was the wisdom this apostolic father was using to build the early Church, and it is still applicable today.

I remember years ago being a part of an international move of God in which there were some really wild demonstrations of the Holy Spirit. The people leading this revival, which became a movement, had taken the position that they would stop nothing. They would allow everything to go unchallenged and undeterred. With this information, I came back home from these meetings. The same things that were happening in their meetings started happening in ours. I adopted the same philosophy that I would stop nothing. Immediately as I prayed, the Lord spoke to me and said, *I never put a river in a garden where I hadn't first put a man there to tend it.*

This was a reference to the river that God put in the Garden of Eden. But first, He had Adam in place to tend and till the Garden. The Lord further told me, *Without a man to take care of My garden, it will produce wild growth that will not allow the maximum fruitfulness.*

I was amazed. I knew that in our situation, I was not to quench the Holy Spirit and His movement, but neither was I to allow things to go unchecked. People could not do whatever they felt they were to do. There had to be protocols for the people to operate in as the Holy Spirit moved. This is what the apostle Paul was setting in place. He was not quenching the Holy Spirit; he was creating boundaries for fruitful growth.

## Protocol 4: Keeping Silent at Times

Protocol number four is *keeping silent at times*. If there is no one to interpret in a service or meeting, then no matter how strong the unction, a tongue should not be given. Paul puts it this way in 1 Corinthians 14:28: "But if there is no interpreter, let him [the one with the tongue] keep silent in church, and let him speak to himself and to God." The idea of speaking "to himself and to God" means that a tongue without interpretation should not be uttered aloud, but it should be held back since it would generate more confusion than help. Also, this means that people are aware of the giftings in their midst and are able to tell if no one is present who carries the gift of interpretation.

The one caveat to this is that the person who is speaking forth a tongue should also pray to interpret it. If someone speaks out a tongue and no one else interprets it, then he or she is responsible for that tongue and its interpretation. This is what 1 Corinthians 14:13 declares: "Therefore let him who speaks in a tongue pray that he may interpret."

Paul is very straightforward about this. Tongues without interpretation are not to be allowed in the Church. Of course, this is not referring to people using their personal prayer language to worship and pray during a service. This refers to those who would use tongues to minister to the whole Church. This is allowed and encouraged—with interpretation. The person who is moved to speak in a tongue in this corporate setting must take ownership of the tongue and make sure it is interpreted. If no one else interprets it, then it is that person's responsibility, so that the Church might be built up without confusion.

In my formative years as a young minister, there was a young man in our church who spoke in tongues frequently in the services. The pastor and the leadership felt this young man had the gifting of varieties of tongues that we spoke about from 1 Corinthians 12:28. Often he would speak in tongues, and then an interpretation would come through someone else. One time, however, he spoke in tongues and no one else interpreted it. We waited for what seemed a very lengthy time (even though it probably was not as long as it seemed in the moment), and it got rather uncomfortable in the room. The pastor then said to the young man, "Do you have the interpretation?"

The young man would not respond. It seemed almost as if he was being stubborn and there was a standoff going on. The pastor then asked him a second time, still with no response.

The pastor then graciously moved on, but everyone knew that what had just happened was out of order. The young man who gave the tongue was responsible for it if no one else interpreted it. This is why the pastor was requiring him to take ownership of it. As uncomfortable as the moment was, it turned into a teaching moment that everyone learned from. The pastor addressed what had happened and taught on it for a few moments. He tried his best not to embarrass or shame the young man, but also to hold him accountable for the tongue he had given.

As often as this young man had spoken in tongues in the services, he had never interpreted. The pastor told me later that he felt God was wanting this young man to move into the interpretation of the tongues he was giving. It seemed this young man's identity was locked up in speaking in tongues, but he did not see himself as one who could or should interpret. He felt interpretation was someone else's job. Scripturally speaking, however, it was his responsibility in the instance when no one was there to do the job. His stubbornness about interpreting could potentially have hindered how God desired to use him.

The bottom line is that if there is no interpreter present, then tongues should not be given. But if they are given, it is then the responsibility of the one who speaks them out to interpret them so that the Church might be edified.

## Protocol 5: Knowing There Is Divine Order

The fifth and final protocol involved in the functioning of tongues and interpretation is to *know there is divine order*. God is a God of divine order. In 1 Corinthians 14:32–33, Paul declares that things are to move in proper arrangement, because "the spirits of the prophets are subject to the prophets. For God is not the author of confusion but of peace, as in all the churches of the saints." Peace is a sign of the Lord's presence, and Paul

*Peace is a sign of the Lord's presence, and Paul makes the astounding statement that the spirits of the prophets are subject to the prophets.*

makes the astounding statement that the spirits of the prophets are subject to the prophets.

People functioning in the gifts can never claim that they were just overwhelmed by the Spirit and were forced to do something. Paul says that no matter how strong the anointing or unction on someone, that person is still in control. Without this understanding, chaos would erupt. Paul makes it blatantly clear that we control the unction or anointing; it does not control us. The Holy Spirit moves with us, and we move with the Holy Spirit. But He will never usurp our will or take over our body.

It is our job to discern the Holy Spirit's movement or stirring and move in agreement with Him. Should something unedifying happen, many times—if not most of the time—this is not the Spirit of God. The Spirit's main operation is to bring edification to us as believers, not strife and confusion. In the course of my life, I have personally had many marvelous and wonderful encounters with the Lord through His Holy Spirit. Never in one of them have I been out of control. I have sensed His presence and have chosen to surrender and give in to what the beckoning of the Spirit is. Yet I was always able at any moment to pull things back and abort what was happening, if the situation demanded. it. The spirit of a person is subject to that person.

## Launching into Uncharted Realms

The Holy Spirit moves through us and magnifies Jesus. May we learn to agree with the Spirit of God. One of the main means through which all of this happens is when we release the unction of His presence in us through the gift of tongues. The flow of the Holy Spirit in us and out of us, like the rivers Jesus spoke of in John 7:37–39, is life changing:

> On the last day, that great day of the feast, Jesus stood and cried out, saying, "If anyone thirsts, let him come to Me and drink. He who believes in Me, as the Scripture has said, out of his heart will flow rivers of living water." But this He spoke concerning the Spirit, whom those believing in Him would receive.

The more I have understood the Holy Spirit we have received, and the more I have understood and operated in the gift of tongues and His other gifts, the more precious all of these have become in my life. Sometimes my understanding has come through learning concepts from the written Word of God. Most of the time, however, it has increased as a result of personal encounters I have had with the Holy Spirit, and through operating in tongues. The Word of God concerning these matters has made sense to me because of my experience with the Lord through these giftings.

> *The more I have understood the Holy Spirit we have received, and the more I have understood and operated in the gift of tongues and His other gifts, the more precious all of these have become in my life.*

I believe the Lord has the same thing for all of us. When the early disciples were filled with the Holy Spirit and spoke in tongues, Peter made this amazing statement in Acts 2:38–39:

> Repent, and let every one of you be baptized in the name of Jesus Christ for the remission of sins; and you shall receive the

gift of the Holy Spirit. For the promise is to you and to your children, and to all who are afar off, as many as the Lord our God will call.

The Holy Spirit and His gifts, including the gift of tongues, is for you, for your children, for those who are far off and for any and all whom Lord will call. No matter how you slice this, that means you and me. We are those whom God desires to empower with these precious gifts. Regarding tongues, we have talked about what the gift of tongues is and what it is not. We have looked at how it operates in us both personally in our private prayer language, and corporately in varieties of tongues that build up and strengthen the Body of Christ. We have seen why we need this powerful gift, and why the Church needs it. We have learned that operating in this gift unlocks mysteries in the spirit realm as God reveals His plans and purposes for us as His representatives on the earth.

In short, hopefully this discussion has educated and inspired us to desire to step into deeper places with the Lord, the Holy Spirit and the operation of His gifts, especially tongues. There are many uncharted realms for us yet to explore in the spiritual dimension, and we will discover them through the Holy Spirit and His manifestation of the gifts in us. May we launch into them by faith and see and experience the glory of God. We will not be disappointed, but we will witness the majesty of our Lord.

# SCRIPTURE INDEX

**Robert Henderson** has had the privilege of traveling the world and preaching the Gospel of the Kingdom. As a bestselling author, TV host, Bible college professor, pastor, apostolic leader and webcast host, he is impacting the globe with the message of the rule of Jesus in lives and in nations.

Robert earned a Doctor of Apostolic Leadership & Applied Theology from Wagner University and leads the Global Prayer and Empowerment Center (GPEC), which is a global house of prayer for the nations. With continental directors on five continents, the center is networking the nations into houses of prayer that can represent their cultures before the Lord.

The passion of Robert's life has always been prayer and intimacy with the Lord. The result of this has been groundbreaking revelation that empowers those in the Body of Christ to step into their ultimate place of rulership and dominion with Jesus.

Robert and his high school sweetheart, Mary, have been married for 43 years. They have six children and seven grandchildren. They make their home in Waco, Texas.

# More from Robert Henderson

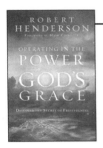

Grounded in Scripture, global apostolic leader Robert Henderson shows how accessible the grace of God is. He identifies the benefits of grace and how it will help you overcome hardship, increase in fruitfulness, live in strength and more. God is ready to pour out His unmerited favor on His children—it is up to us to be willing to receive it.

*Operating in the Power of God's Grace*